HEALIN
BY CHAN..... YOUR MIND

A SPIRITUAL AND HUMOROUS APPROACH
TO ACHIEVING HAPPINESS

DR. JEFFREY L. GURIAN

HAPPINESS CENTER PUBLICATIONS

NEW YORK, NEW YORK

ABOUT THE AUTHOR

A T THE TENDER age of only 7 or 8 years old, Jeffrey Gurian already knew he could take away certain types of pain with his hands. He used it on himself and his little sister Ronnie. It came naturally to him. Years later that experience opened him up to the concept of past lives, because when little children intuitively know something that no one taught them, it makes sense that it could have come from a previous existence. Jeffrey refers to these ideas as "comforting thoughts!"

His original training was as a Cosmetic Dentist and he received his D.D.S. degree from Temple University School of Dentistry, and in later years worked as an Assoc. Clinical Professor at New York University College of Dentistry in the Oral Medicine/Oro-Facial Pain Department.

His specialty was treating the physical symptoms of stress-related illness like Migraine-type headaches, neck, shoulder, and back pain, Vertigo, dizziness, light headedness, ear pain, Tinnitus (ringing in the ears), and many other symptoms often related to a TMJ (Tempero-Mandibular Joint) dysfunction caused by clenching and grinding of the teeth.

In 1999 he was made a Board member of The Association for Spirituality and Psychotherapy, where he still serves, and has lectured at Energy Psychology Conferences in the US and Canada on his techniques of "Energy Healing", and "Spiritual Healing" using a very gentle technique of "talk and touch" he developed which he calls "STAR Therapy", an acronym for Spiritual, Trans-formational, Affirmative, Resonance Therapy."

It's a way of learning to change the way you think to release "heart wounds", as he calls them, and physical body pain through a "Body-Mind-Spirit" approach to achieving Happiness and Well Being!

He used it on himself to "change his own mind" and cure himself of a severe stutter, which he suffered with into his twenties and beyond, because learning to change the way you think can be used to overcome many obstacles we face in life.

This is his first book, and he's excited for you to take this journey with him.

EDITORIAL REVIEWS

"This very special and beautiful healing book is the distillation of a lifetime of wisdom from the master healer Jeffrey Gurian. The book teaches us, using the many techniques that Gurian has developed, that all healing originates from the heart—and to convey this timeless truth, he is not afraid to stand naked in front of us as readers, and speak directly from his personal vulnerability directly to our hearts. This book is a gift."

—Kenneth Porter, M.D., Ordained Diamond Approach Teacher/Minister and former President, Association for Spirituality and Psychotherapy

"Dr. Gurian uses a wonderful openness about himself to help us see and understand ourselves. Without judgment, his openness helps us be freer to be open about ourselves, seeing it all as an opportunity for growth. This is an important book to distinguish spirituality from religion, and presents powerful tools we can use for healing, health and happiness."

—Dr. Henry Grayson, Ph.D. Author of *The New Physics of Love* and *Your Power to Heal*, and Founder of The National Institute of the Psychotherapies.

"Without a doubt, Jeffrey Gurian poured his heart and soul into this book. He is an amazingly accomplished person in areas that didn't seem connected until I read his book "Healing Your Heart By Changing Your Mind." It is the path that Dr. Gurian created that allowed him to combine the fields of medicine, humor and much more. He offers an angle in which you can reside in happiness and reach your highest potential despite outer circumstances. I love that he is a doctor so he isn't just satisfied to give us an often overplayed example like in many other self-help books. He offers a solid reasoning while keeping the book light and fun. "Healing Your Heart By Changing Your Mind" is a brilliantly written book that deserves to be a handbook to all of us happiness-seeking human beings."

—Otakara Klettke, international best-selling author of *Hear Your Body Whisper; How to Unlock Your Self-Healing Mechanism.*

"Dr. Gurian is a master of so many disciplines, including being a brilliant humorist, the pressure probably caused his own heart attack. Lucky for us, his genius helps us minimize our risk and live healthier after an episode like that. He's on my speed dial along with God."

—Richard Lewis—Actor/Comedian/Author

"Who said mindset is no laughing matter? It can be when approached from a healing perspective. This book will open your heart to how the power of smiling and humor, and not taking yourself too seriously, can change your mindset taking your attitude toward life in a more positive direction. Get your hands on this book if you are looking for a proven way to achieve healing at the heart level with a twist of humor!"

—Christopher Salem/America's Prosperity Coach (Prosperneur) and International Keynote Speaker—Award Winning Author of *Master Your Inner Critic—Resolve the Root Cause,* and *Mastering the Art of Success* with Jack Canfield.

"As CEO & Executive Director of a spiritually-based treatment program in Fort Lauderdale, Florida, I highly recommend this amazing book by Jeffrey Gurian. His combination of spirituality and humor is a very effective methodology for positive change, and is an inspiration to me and countless others in and out of recovery."

—Ray Rapaglia—Exec. Director of James Club Recovery

Jeffrey@JeffreyGurian.com

"Jeffrey writes with a clarity and sincere openness as he presents tools to help the reader embrace their sensitivity. This book is like a spiritual GPS to guide his readers into depth and purpose by simplifying life's complexities into workable steps of practical wisdom. It's a handbook to guide people on their soul journey. A fun, practical book people can understand and easily apply to life".

—Marcy Calhoun, Internationally Acclaimed Psychic and best selling author of *Are You Really Too Sensitive* and *Do You Really Have A Choice*

"Jeffrey Gurian looks to bring lightness and laughter to everyone he meets. Plus he has met everyone in comedy from the old Catskills comics to a kid who does open mics in Brooklyn."

—Ron Bennington—Host of The Bennington Show on Sirius XM

"Jeffrey Gurian gives us an overview about the nature of consciousness and one man's journey to understanding the depth of his heart. The perennial knowledge offered is a guide for all spiritual seekers on the path to self discovery.

HEALING YOUR HEART, BY CHANGING YOUR MIND gives us the tools of awareness, the wisdom of feeling and the light hearted optimism to get one through even the most dire situation. What so many other writers have attempted to do: merge the heart and mind into one complete whole—Jeffrey does beautifully! He is now loved the world over for his sharp witted sense of humor and his gentle caring spirit."

—Alan Steinfeld, founder of New Realities

"As a person who has been clean and sober for more than 26 years, I find this book to be remarkably helpful. In his own inimitable way, Dr. Gurian delivers a spiritual message of hope and recovery with humor. It's an enjoyable stroll down memory lane."

—Peter Santoro Vice-President
Lower Eastside Service Center

"There are many powerful concepts in this book that I think many people can benefit from. Lots of these ideas fit very well with our teachings, namely the power of thought and speech, having positive thoughts, and that saying positive things will create positive situations. Believing and accepting that all that happens is divine providence is also a key factor in our teachings. I personally gained a lot from it, and believe you will too."

—Rabbi Shmary Gurary, Director of Development,
Bnos Menachem School for Girls

TABLE OF CONTENTS

AN INTRODUCTORY
MESSAGE TO MY READERS

WELCOME TO MY book. I'm truly grateful you have decided to read it. I wrote this book for all the people like myself who have been wounded in their hearts.

I can only hope that my own personal experience can serve to benefit you in some meaningful way, for as they say, a smart man learns from his own mistakes, but a wise man learns from others.

That's not to say that you or I ever really made any mistakes, because the Spiritual approach teaches us that we were supposed to do every single thing we ever did in our lives, whether it feels like a mistake or not, . . . but I'll address that more as we progress.

This book is based on a simple premise, . . . from the time you were a child, every single time someone lied to you, or broke a promise to you, humiliated or embarrassed you, broke up with you, cheated on you, or hurt your feelings in any way, it wounded you deeply in your heart. Not on a physical plane, but on a meta-physical, energetic plane, which can be just as damaging, if not more-so.

The scrapes and bruises of your childhood have long since healed, however, the emotional wounds, and the wounds to your heart are still there, . . . deeply embedded, alive, and doing damage.

Not only have they survived, they have, and still are, influencing every relationship you've ever had, and every decision you've ever made, often blocking you in your quest for Happiness.

Heart wounds stay with you until they're released. That's what the concept of Healing is all about, . . . opening the blockages, and releasing the wounds, and the negative energy that is trapped inside of us, to restore the flow of energy, . . . our Universal Life Force, . . . to every cell in our bodies, and every fibre of our beings.

The wounds you suffer at a young age, from one to six, during your so-called "formative years" may stay with you for your entire life, unless you find a way to release them, and let them go.

During those tender years, when your personality was forming, your mind was like a clean slate. You were so impressionable, so open, vulnerable, and sensitive, that the wounds you received were deeply imprinted into your consciousness. Indelibly etched, . . . if you will, . . . into your "heart-consciousness."

It's as if your heart, and every cell, organ and system in your body is it's own separate entity, with it's own consciousness. And that is true. Every single part of your body has it's own consciousness, with a memory all to it's own!

It's not an easy task to rid yourself of these wounds, and release yourself from their power, but it's certainly not impossible. It just takes knowledge, . . . specifically what I like to call "new information." New information is necessary to acquire, because of one of the most important principles that this book is based on, . . . "you can not get better with the same mind that got you sick."

That is a point I will keep coming back to throughout the course of this book, because it's important to realize that your own best thinking got you into every "bad" situation you've ever been in.

Each time you were stuck in an uncomfortable spot in your life, you can rest assured that you got yourself into it utilizing your best thinking. Then you figured out what to do about it, by also using your best thinking.

If the outcome was less than desirable, as it often is, and if that seems to be a pattern in your life, then it's important that you reach the conclusion that you can not count on your best thinking to guide you, because your best thinking is flawed.

Interestingly enough, your best thinking is based on information compiled from your past experience. What else have we got to use? We can't use someone else's past as a guide, although that wouldn't be a bad idea. It would basically be the equivalent of learning from someone else's experience.

However, most of us are reluctant to do that, because we tell ourselves, "this might not have worked for all those other people, but I'm different. I can pull it off." That's our ego spinning off out of control. Our ego tells us that millions of other people are wrong, and that only we are right.

So, honoring our collective weakness as people in being able to learn from someone else's mistakes, and keeping with the concept of using our own past as our guide, the next thought should make perfect sense to you. Obviously, you can not change your past. The only thing you can change is how you view it. You can only change your perspective of your past.

In order to do that, you need to draw on this "new information," and therefore must also change your "database", so to speak, . . . the place from which you draw your information. You need to fill it up, or re-program it, with this new information, . . . which is basically Spiritual Wisdom, leading to a whole new perspective, and a new positive worldview. In doing so, you can literally "change your mind."

In accomplishing that, you give yourself the opportunity to release these gnawing, insidious, damaging heart wounds you have been carrying all these years, that have been ruining your relationships, influencing your decisions, and have been making you physically and emotionally ill.

I'll be discussing this concept at length throughout the book, but realizing that the problem lies partially with you is a very important step.

For instance, if you keep on having the same bad relationship with different people, where the details are the same, and the only thing that changes are the names, it's important to realize that the only common denominator in all those relationships has been you.

It isn't possible that all of those people who don't even know each other got together to conspire against you. In each and every one of those relationships, only *you* keep turning up.

Unfortunately for me, I'm more than qualified to have written this book because, as I mentioned earlier, I too have been wounded in my heart. The ideas and techniques I discuss in this book, are the ideas and techniques I have had to use in my own life in order to help me release my own heart wounds, so that I could begin to accomplish the things I was meant to accomplish. This book was one of them.

I had to learn to incorporate many new concepts into my life to help reduce my own stress, so that I could make some sense out of what I was going through, and better understand the events that had occurred.

For example, one of the most important concepts I ever had to learn was the one I mentioned earlier in talking about "mistakes." I had to understand that every single thing that ever happened to me, even, . . . or should I say "especially", the things I thought were bad, happened exactly the way they were supposed to.

If I hadn't had to suffer every single one of the heart wounds I received, and been given the Grace to survive them, I wouldn't be exactly who or where I am right now, at this very moment in time.

Not one single thing in my life could have changed, or else every other thing in my life would have changed as well.

For example, there have been times in my life when I didn't want to be me. At those times, although I might not have realized it then, I was engaging in self-hatred. One of my own personal realities is that I have been blessed with two amazing daughters that mean the world to me. They were given to me by the woman who was their mother, and my wife.

It took me a long time to realize that if I had been anyone else, . . . as I had often wished I was, . . . or been even *slightly* different, I might not ever have met the woman who gave me the things that are the most dear to me in the entire world, . . . my two daughters. That woman was attracted to me exactly the way I was, and if I had been any different, who knows what might have happened.

I may have had other children, or I may never have had the opportunity to even have children. There are no guarantees in life. But the one thing that is for sure is that without my ex-wife's DNA it certainly couldn't have been *those* two children, the ones that make my heart fill with joy. Although we weren't able to stay together, I will be eternally grateful to her for giving me that gift.

In one sense, nothing in life ever really has to happen. When you have somewhere to go, you could always leave your house one minute earlier or later than you actually do, and in doing that you have to realize that the whole rest of your life changes. Sometimes not in dramatic ways, but it's always going to be different.

It's similar to the concept that every time you make either a right turn or a left turn, your whole life is different, mainly because everyone else in the world is in a different position at that moment.

Just think of how many times you just catch someone by one second before they leave the house, or conversely, just miss someone by a minute when you call on the phone, or you run into someone you didn't expect to see, solely because you were late to go somewhere else, or a bicycle, or speeding car misses you by a fraction of an inch as you begin to step off the curb. You can easily miss a plane by a minute. One tiny minute earlier or later can easily change your life.

When you leave the location you're in right now, you can conceivably travel in any direction, and each different way you could possibly go, different things would happen. But you can not allow yourself to dwell on that, or try and second-guess it, because you'll literally drive yourself crazy. It seems very haphazard but it's not. You just have to know that whichever way you choose to go is the way you were supposed to go, no matter what the consequences. You are always being guided.

About a week after I wrote this last paragraph, I was driving home from visiting my Mom. I hadn't seen her for a couple of weeks, even though we speak almost every day, but she sounded like she needed some company so I went to visit her. On the way home, I was side-swiped by a bus. I remember it very clearly as I was very present for it.

I heard this loud sound, and as I looked out my window, I felt my car bouncing off the side of the bus, and watched my sideview mirror being torn off, and I sat there waiting for the pain. Fortunately it didn't come. I was fine. Just car damage.

I never thought for a minute, why did this have to happen. I understood the principles involved. The time I left my mother's house was very arbitrary. I could easily have left a minute sooner or later, or five minutes, or an hour. It was totally up to me.

There was a time in my life when I would have thought, "if I had only left a few minutes earlier or later, I wouldn't have gotten hit by the bus", and obsessed over it, driving myself crazy.

Now I understand that getting hit by that bus, may have kept me from getting into a worse accident a little further down the road, by keeping me exactly where I was for an extra half hour. My Higher Power, who is always watching over me decided that for whatever reason, beyond my comprehension, I had to be delayed, without getting hurt. Many people get hit by a bus and get hurt. Fortunately, I wasn't one of those people.

The bus driver seemed shocked that I was so calm. I lent him my pen and a piece of paper so that he could write down his information for me. I was very grateful throughout the whole thing, because I was very aware of all the other possible ways it could have played out. This represented a new way of thinking for me.

I was very aware that it didn't have to end up the way it did. I understood all the possibilities of how it could have worked out. It wasn't my time.

Another time, I got stuck in the elevator of my high-rise apartment building on a Sunday afternoon, when I was on my way to go to an event that started at a certain time.

I didn't have time to get stuck in an elevator, especially on a day when it's difficult to get repairmen to come out.

I also hadn't realized until that moment that that was a fear of mine, getting stuck on a high floor in an elevator.

I pressed the alarm button and informed the doorman that I was stuck. He said he'd call for help and that I should just try and remain calm. He said that because it was a Sunday, it might take a while, but that he'd stay in touch with me, and would try to do whatever he could.

I sat down on the floor, closed my eyes, and just started to meditate. In about 20 minutes or so the elevator started to move. It went down only one floor and I got out, instead of waiting to see if it would go all the way down to the lobby.

I took another elevator to the lobby and when I asked the doorman what he had done to get it started again, he said he didn't do anything, that it just started up on it's own. He was mystified!

So instead of cursing my luck, because getting stuck in the elevator made me late, I thought to myself that maybe I wasn't meant to get to the street for another 20 minutes, and perhaps getting stuck in the elevator saved me from some sort of catastrophe.

That type of thinking involved me "changing my mind", because there was a time that when something like that happened I would have thought of myself as an unlucky victim!

I have many more stories like that which I will share with you during the course of this book, but suffice it to say that I came to realize that every single thing that ever happened to me in my life, whether I choose to label it good or bad, had to happen in the exact way that it did, in order for every other thing to happen, including for me to have been exactly where I was on the night when I met the woman who was to become the mother of my children.

Although we got divorced, she went on to re-marry, and had three other children besides the two she had with me. In retrospect, I now see that those children needed to be born, and the only way that could have happened is for my marriage to have broken up.

With all the pain and sadness it produced, it also produced a home for those three children, two of whom were adopted, and needed a loving home like the one they are in. The one thing I could always say about my ex-wife was that she was an excellent mother.

I will also say that because of the principles in this book, we are on very good terms. I have been welcome in her home for years, and often go there to celebrate holidays at one big dinner with what I consider to be my whole "extended family." I consider her husband a friend of mine. We all planned both of my daughter's weddings together.

When my father was deathly ill, my ex-wife visited him in the hospital, and called my mother frequently to see how she was doing. When my Dad was still well, she brought her new babies to visit both of my parents, and my Dad truly loved her little girl. He used to look forward to her visits.

Those are the kinds of things that are only possible by incorporating certain principles into your life. By ridding your life of resentment, and anger, . . . by ridding your life of the waste of time of living in the past thinking about what you "should have done," and what you "could have done." Remember that amazing saying,

"Yesterday is history, tomorrow's a mystery, today is a gift, and that's why they call it 'the present'."

I didn't always think that way. It wasn't because I didn't want to. I just didn't know any better.

The important thing to realize is that you are not on this quest for knowledge and truth alone. There are millions more like you who are on the same journey, and more starting every day. As we learn, and change, we become powers of example for others, and carry the message to others in pain.

In terms of the experiences that wounded you, the spiritual approach teaches us that we are all the same. Although we all look different, we can all identify with certain feelings and experiences, because on some level we are truly all the same.

There are only so many things that a human being can experience. Once we accept that fact, we begin to understand that there's nothing so bad, or so damaging that you could have gone through, that no one else has experienced also.

My plan, in the course of this book, is to try and share with you some of the difficult things I have encountered and overcome in my own life. I have found that whenever I could find the courage to share something either difficult for me to say, or that I found embarrassing, because it exposed something deeply personal inside of me, I was able to get better. You will find the same thing, if you can allow yourself to trust the process.

Whenever I am given the courage to share something I find embarrassing to admit, I always notice that I'm the only one who's embarrassed. I'm the only one who turns red, or whose hands are clammy. That may happen to *you* when you share something personal, but it doesn't happen to you when *I* do. Except if you're an empath, like I've been told I am. The chapters on owning your sensitivity will teach you how to handle things like that, so that you don't "overfeel" your feelings.

Hopefully the path that I have traveled, and the difficulties I have managed to overcome, simply, (or not so simply) by changing my thoughts, can help make your trip a little bit easier, and help you to overcome the adversities in your own lives.

Writing a book like this, and imparting Spiritual Wisdom carries a big responsibility. Knowledge is power, and it can be abused. It is also a great responsibility. Once you own knowledge, you are responsible for that knowledge. You can never truly say you didn't know it. You can choose to ignore it if you wish, because we were given Free Will, but you can never truly say you didn't know.

As I progressed further and further along my path, I developed an insatiable thirst for knowledge, and truth. I read the works of many people who write in this field, and who I credit at the end of this book. I also read the works of ancient masters, who immersed themselves in esoteric wisdom, and I can honestly say that there's only so much knowledge in the world.

Let me clarify what I mean by that. Each person adds their own particular slant to the information, but it's all there already. It's all been said before. Therefore, it's not so much what you learn by reading each book, it's what it re-affirms to you. The Spiritual approach says that all the knowledge you need is already inside of you. You were born with it.

It also says, "When the student is ready, the teacher will appear," meaning that all it takes is for someone to say something to you that strikes a familiar chord within you, and stirs you to learn more. It "resonates" as a truth inside of your heart.

G-d doesn't speak to us directly. He speaks to us through other people. He puts other people in our path during the course of our day, to give us needed information. They're the people we run into unexpectedly, or the people we meet for the first time who tell us something we really needed to hear.

These people are there to give us guidance, and information that we need to carry on in our lives. They have no idea that they are G-d's messengers. They are just going about their day like you and I, until The Universe enables them to cross our paths.

In that same vein, hopefully something I say can direct you to something inside of you that you need to get in touch with. That is the true excitement of writing a book like this.

In writing about such matters, there is a great need to be in touch with your purpose, to check your intentions, to examine your motivation, and to deliver the information with as much humility as possible. The writer can never seek to be more important than the message, for truly the writer is but a vehicle, or a channel for carrying the message.

The inherent danger in discussing your humility, is that you lose it at the same time you're discussing it. It's in an inverse proportion. The more you discuss your humility, the less humility you wind up with. I have a friend named Arthur, who, when discussing humility in general, would laughingly say as a joke about himself, "No one has more humility than I do."

Anyway, I'm glad I can be there to accompany you on your journey, and possibly aid you in some small way in your quest for Knowledge, Truth, and Happiness.

Sending you lots of light and heart energy! See you on every page.

Sincerely,

Jeffrey Gurian

ABOUT THE TITLE

ONE OF THE hardest things about writing a book is finding just the right title. Not only the *right* title, but a title that encompasses in a nutshell, everything you want to say and more, and on top of that is catchy, and possibly even humorous as well. I labored over it for weeks. I wrote endless possibilities, trying to incorporate several messages, so that people would know exactly what this book was about, just by hearing the title.

I almost picked **"If It's Not Fun, I Don't Want To Be There"**, because one of the major themes of this book is about our unfulfilled need to have fun, and how we must try and make everything in our lives fun, creating our own little "Happiness Centers™" for ourselves in the process.

But that didn't touch on the Spirituality, or the Healing themes of the book. Then I thought of titles, and sub-titles that were strictly humorous like:

Take My Advice – I'm Not Using It Anyway; How To Be Happy and Make Your Life Perfect

Play Your Way To Health and Happiness While Creating A Daycare Center For Your Inner Child

I Was Having A Perfectly Good Day, 'Till I Tried To Make It Better

I happen to like the sound of all of them, but again, none of them quite seemed to encapsulate all that I wanted to say. The one I finally settled on is absolutely nothing like the others, however it seemed to come the closest to including all the points I wanted to make, the most important of which are that we are highly sensitive, Spiritual beings who often suffer with stress related physical and mental illness due to that very same sensitivity we are gifted with.

We internalize our stress. We absorb it from our environment as if our bodies were like sponges. It blocks the flow of our universal life force, and it affects us deeply on a "heart level".

Not so much in terms of heart disease as we know it, but energetically, . . . on an *energy* level, our fourth Chakras become wounded. Those "heart wounds" need to be "released" before we can heal. My intent is to help guide you in reaching that goal.

THE DIFFERENCE BETWEEN RELIGION AND SPIRITUALITY

A T FIRST GLANCE you might wonder about the connection between the heart and the mind, and what part "Spirituality" could possibly play in treating mental and emotional illness, as well as the physical pain and symptoms that often accompany that diagnosis.

First, it is important to understand my use of the term "Spirituality". Contrary to what many people think, it has nothing to do with religion. Religion can be a wonderful thing, but by its very nature, it tends to divide people by putting them into a category, . . .

automatically putting other people outside of that category, . . . while Spirituality brings people of all backgrounds together.

To me, Spirituality is simply the belief in a Higher Power of your own understanding, . . . an all-loving Higher Power, that is there to help and guide you when you truly need it. Some people call this Higher Power "G-d", others refer to it as "Nature", or "The Universe."

Some people even think of G-d as an acronym for Good Orderly Direction. It doesn't matter what you call it, as long as you acknowledge that it isn't you! You don't make the sun rise or set, the moon come out at night, the seasons change, or the tides come in and out. Those things are ruled by a Force beyond our comprehension. It is the Force behind all that happens, and behind all Healing in the world as well.

The power of Spirituality is the reason why the 12-step programs are the only thing that is so effective in dealing with any kind of substance abuse.

In terms of physical damage, anywhere between 50 and 150 million people in this country alone suffer with chronic stress related illness, . . . Migraine Headaches, neck, back, and shoulder pain, dizziness, Vertigo, and the type of Depression often associated with being ill over a long period of time. These and other symptoms often do not seem to have a precise medical cause.

Very often, there is also a tie in with a Tempero-Mandibular Joint (TMJ) dysfunction caused by excessive stress-related clenching and grinding of the teeth, which can lead not only to the above-mentioned symptoms but also to Tinnitus, chronic fatigue, jaw pain, ear pain, and hearing loss as well. For various reasons, many of these patients go undiagnosed.

This is where my "unusual" background comes in to play. Most books of this kind are written by people with Ph.D. or M.D. after their names. The letters following my name are D.D.S., because my original training was as a Cosmetic Dentist. Dentists, however are in the unique position of using the power of touch to help them build their practices, and to build confidence in their patients. I'll explain the connection in a moment.

Psychiatrists and psychologists are taught never to touch their patients. Dentists, as I said, rely on touch to build their practices. Not only do we touch, but we touch and hold your head, where all your thoughts and feelings come from.

People always vote dentists as professionals they trust. As a matter of fact, most people would more easily change physicians than dentists once they find one they trust. All good dentists are also psychologists. We have to be, in order to make such a diverse population of patients feel comfortable, especially when so many of them are burdened with deep-seated fears of going to the dentist.

My background also qualifies me to treat the physical symptoms of stress-related illness and Depression with Healing Through Touch, namely the TMJ associated Migraine headaches, and head, neck, and shoulder pain associated with clenching and grinding the teeth.

Depressed people need touch to help re-connect them to their inner strength, and to the world around them. All living things need touch and attention. If babies don't receive enough touch, they fail to thrive, and may not survive.

People with chronic stress-related illness live in a world of negativity. They interpret everything that happens to them in their lives as a negative event, or as some form of "punishment."

They perceive themselves as "victims". They are often superstitious, and are prone to remarks like, "Well with my luck, such-and such will happen", which can easily become a self-fulfilling prophecy.

Most of these people have experienced a great deal of psychological and emotional pain in their lives, and have become overwhelmed by it. From a psycho-spiritual point of view, they've been "wounded on a heart level". Some are literally "heart-broken."

They often feel that they are too sensitive, and that their sensitivity works against them.

They must be taught how to "own" their sensitivity, and use it as the strength it's meant to be, and not the weakness they interpret it to be. It is important to note that those on a Spiritual path seek to become more sensitive, not less.

If not cared for, these sensitive, overwhelmed, depressed people can become suicidal. By the time they find someone who truly understands their problem, they may have been searching for help for years, gradually losing hope, until they have none left. They literally become "hope-less". They become disconnected from their spiritual essence, from their lives, and from the people around them.

In order to be helped, they need to be re-connected with "Spirit", and healed "on a heart level". When people are that depressed, all the TMJ appliances and medications in the world are not going to be enough. They may help to alleviate some symptoms, but they only take care of the "body" part of the "body-mind-spirit" equation.

Traditional psychotherapy may also help heal the Depression, but that still only takes care of the "body-mind" part of the equation.

What makes the difference in treating people struggling with the severe Depression that often accompanies the above-mentioned stress-related symptoms is the incorporation of a Spiritual factor.

A Spiritual approach is most effective when patients have gotten to the point where they are open and willing to accept "new information" in their lives. As I explained in the Introduction, this "new information", which is basically Spiritual Wisdom, is critically important, because of the principle I stressed earlier, . . . **you can not get better with the same mind that got you sick.**

You can not use your "current mindset", or information that you already "own" to think your way out of the situation you're in.

The problem is that very often, new information is "scary" to us. We don't even know where to file it, because we have no folder for it on our mental "hard drives."

The older we get, the more reluctant we are to try anything new, for several reasons. Some of us feel we've gotten this far doing what we've been doing, and so to change, challenges every belief we've ever held in the past. It would in effect negate many of our previous choices, which were based on our old mindset. That is a difficult thing for many people to handle.

New paradigms make us uncomfortable, because they don't relate to anything we already know. The word "new" makes that a given.

It's like change. Many people avoid change even if they're miserable, fearing that the new thing might be even worse than what they already have. Therefore they stay where they are, often living in misery, for fear of who they might become.

I remember very clearly, before I stopped stuttering, which I will be talking about throughout this book, I was very nervous, because as much as I hated being a stutterer, it was so much a part of my identity, that once I stopped, who would I be?

Despite our reluctance to change, we must learn to confront our fears, and in doing so, allow ourselves to experience something new in our quest to change our lives. That "something new" is Spiritual Principles and Spiritual Wisdom.

"STAR" THERAPY—
HEALING ON A HEART LEVEL

"STAR" THERAPY IS an acronym I created that stands for Spiritual, Transformational, Affirmative, Resonance Therapy. It's a body-mind-spirit technique, a gentle system of "talk-and-touch", done within the context of a Guided Meditation with music. I use it to strengthen people "on a heart level."

While experiencing very gentle "Healing Thru Touch" techniques, like Shiatsu, Reiki, Applied Kinesiology, Therapeutic Touch, Chakra Balancing, Cranio-Sacral Work, and Intuitive Healing, along with Visualization, and the use of Affirmations, the patient is exposed to Spiritually uplifting messages, and Spiritual Wisdom, geared towards helping them deal with the particular problems they are facing.

The combination serves to open up blocked energy pathways to allow the flow of our Universal Life Force, (Chi, Ki, Prana), and to help the patient release their "heart wounds." It leaves them with a deep-seated sense of Happiness and Well-Being.

Basically, by using energy, or touch therapy, I take out "the bad stuff", and replace it with "good stuff". It's a physical principle that two things cannot occupy the same space at the same time, so in order to make space inside of your heart, and mind for the "good thoughts", and "good energy", we have to first get rid of the "bad thoughts", and the "bad energy".

As I explained, it's done during the context of a guided meditation during which I am giving the patient new thoughts, and new information, while using Healing music as Resonance Therapy. Our bodies "resonate" to certain frequencies. When you're happy, your body is resonating, or vibrating at a higher frequency than when you're sad.

The "Resonance" part of "STAR" Therapy refers not only to the music, and to the sound of my voice hopefully coming through my Heart Chakra, but to the fact that certain information resonates as a truth inside of the individual who needs to be healed.

It's based on the Spiritual concept that we're all born with all of the knowledge we need inside of us already, but we're not in touch with it.

Then someone you meet either says or does something that puts you in touch with that information, and it feels comfortable to you, as if you already knew it, . . . because you did! It resonates inside of you as a truth, and you can begin using it in your thinking process, as part of your armamentarium of thoughts.

It's not so much what you learned, but what was re-affirmed to you.

I always use the exact same music with each patient, each time that I see them. I try and create a repeatable environment so that the room and everything in it gets imprinted into the person's Cellular Memory, as a positive experience that can be repeated.

Their bodies get accustomed to hearing that music, and thanks to Cellular Memory, they go into an automatic state of relaxation as soon as they do.

Their bodies also get used to everything else in my workplace as well. Because my space is a "Happiness Center™", then everything that they see and hear there is geared towards making them feel Happy.

When they see, and experience the exact same things over, and over again while they are in a state of extreme relaxation and trust, it becomes imprinted inside of them, in their hearts, and deeply into their subconscious minds. When that happens, their Cellular Memory can go back to that experience when it is triggered to do so.

I teach them how to trigger it automatically, on their own. In the case I mentioned, the music becomes one of the triggers in changing Cellular Memory, and creating new neural pathways.

This technique, accompanied by the use of affirmations, which explains the "Affirmative" part of "STAR" Therapy, allows them to strengthen themselves both mentally and physically, by re-connecting them to their Spiritual core, and effectively re-programming their subconscious mind.

Affirmations are positive thoughts meant to be repeated over and over again, sort of like brain washing yourself to think differently. I used Affirmations a lot in order to cure myself of Stuttering.

It is this re-programming of thought, with the new information, . . . the Spiritual Wisdom, . . . that enables people to heal on a "heart level." It affords them a new set of tools, and a different way of thinking, and processing information, that they can use whenever they feel overwhelmed by certain life events. That explains the "Transformational" part of "STAR" Therapy.

It truly is a "Transformation" and it occurs rather quickly if you are able to really embrace these principles, and incorporate them into your thinking and into your life.

It's particularly effective with symptoms such as Migraine Headaches, Head, Neck and Upper Back Pain. It's also great for associated symptoms like Tinnitus, (ringing in the ears), Chronic Fatigue, Vertigo, ear pain, hearing loss, and the Depression that often accompanies these things, along with other physical discomforts, which unknowingly are most often caused by a TMJ (Jaw Joint) imbalance in people who don't know that they're grinding and clenching their teeth.

That's how my unusual background as a dentist, with 30 years of experience treating patients comes in handy. It has helped me to develop this theory after having been able to help so many people, by making sense out of their symptoms.

Most people writing, and working in this field are either M.D.'s or Ph.D's who don't have much experience working in the mouth.

The Tempero-Mandibular Joint is considered a "master joint" controlling not only the movement of your jaw, but also how the rest of your body feels.

It's the reason that many athletes, . . . especially football players, wrestlers, and weight lifters, where strength is key, . . . wear appliances on their teeth known as MORA Appliances, . . . Mandibular Orthognathic Repositioning Appliances, . . . (developed by internationally known TMJ specialist Dr. Michael Gelb, who I lectured for while at N.Y.U.), because theoretically if you open the jaw to the correct position, it will increase your physical strength.

Conversely, if your teeth are worn down, or if your jaw is in an incorrect position, your physical strength will diminish, leading to the above symptoms, as well as weakness and Depression.

The search for the elusive state of Happiness is the cause of a great deal of stress-related illness. An example of the "new information" that is used to help patients change their perspective, is that "Happiness is not something to be sought. Happiness is the byproduct of leading your life in a certain way, . . . a Spiritual way."

Many of us grow up thinking that the right car, the right job, the right spouse, or the right amount of money will make us happy. Sometimes life allows us to achieve those goals, and we find that we're still not happy. As a matter of fact, very often we're miserable with the thought of all we have, and that it's still not making us happy. Leading your life according to Spiritual principles will automatically make you happy. You don't have to seek it. It will find you.

Another definition of Happiness that I like is: "Happiness is wanting what you already have."

So if it is possible that in dealing with stress-related illness, our subconscious mind has made the decision for us to get sick in the first place, then in recovering from such stress-related illness, we are often in essence "arguing with our own minds".

In my own personal case of conquering stuttering, part of my journey was in convincing my subconscious mind that I did not "need" to stutter, and that it was no longer necessary for me to stutter.

It is only by including G-d and Spirituality in our recovery, along with "STAR" Therapy, that we can win that argument, by changing our thinking enough to heal us on all levels, . . . heart, body, mind, and spirit.

MY STORY

MY HEART HAS been wounded, more times than I can count. More times than I'd care to remember. Since I was a little boy, I have been deceived, lied to, embarrassed, humiliated, broken up with, cheated on, taken advantage of, and betrayed.

The worst part was that very often these wounds were inflicted upon me by people who supposedly "loved" me, and by people I trusted.

If people who "love" you treat you that way, what can you expect from the rest of the world? Take the simplest example. Divorce. How many people do you know who are divorced? Now stop and think for a second that every single person who is divorced was once married. It sounds so simple.

By definition, you can not get divorced without having first been married. And every single person who got married truly believed, . . . or at least I hope they did, . . . that it would last forever.

So they get married, and some of them think they're happy, because they're living in their own movie, as each of us are, and suddenly one day, they're in the middle of a painful divorce. Is there any other kind?

Think about this for a minute. If you ever had a special someone in your life, who was the one person you thought you could trust, and over time, you finally let down the walls, and opened up to them, and told them every deep dark secret about yourself as a human being, . . . your wants, your fears, your desires, . . . and suddenly one day not only do they leave you, but they use all this privileged information you gave them against you, how do you ever trust anyone again?

In a case like that, the heart wounds are incredibly deep. But we can not allow an experience like that to cause us to isolate and lose trust in the whole of humanity. That would be giving the person that hurt us entirely too much power. We need then to work on releasing those heart wounds.

In my own case, I knew I needed to release my heart wounds, because they weakened me, causing me to make wrong decisions, and to wallow in self-pity. In my own mind, . . . or in my own little movie in my mind, . . . which is how I like to think of it, I was always "the victim." The Universe often seemed to be conspiring against me.

As an aside, it's important to acknowledge that we're all living our own little movies in our mind. We star in them, cast them, and we tirelessly raise the funds needed to shoot them. In that sense we are true producers.

The problem for me was that I was invariably on the wrong page of the script, and there was never a director around to yell out "Cut" when I needed him. The movie often ended in disaster. It was one Irwin Allen special after the other. (For those of you old enough to remember "The Master of Disaster!"

I know they say that G-d doesn't give you more than you can handle, . . . but sometimes He comes awfully close. I feel like I've had many obstacles to overcome in my life. But, I must never again allow myself to think I was a victim, because I wasn't, and I'm not. Hard as it is to admit, I often volunteered for the pain.

I have also been wounded in my heart by total strangers to whom I gave away my power, by letting their words, and judgments affect me, and weaken me. But again, no matter what it may sound like, I do not consider myself a victim now, nor was I ever a victim.

When cruel, unthinking people chose to inflict their negativity onto me, I absorbed it like a sponge, and took it into my heart. It remained painfully lodged there for too many years. As hard as I've worked, some traces of it may still remain. Those heart wounds affected every choice I ever made in my life.

In my early years, before I knew better, I *thought* I was a victim. A victim of other people's cruelty. Looking for my part in it was difficult. How could I possibly have had any part in people being cruel to me? I didn't know then what I know now. I wouldn't have been ready for it even if I had. I couldn't have handled it then.

Knowledge is not only power, but it is responsibility, and you must know how to use it, and be ready to handle it, or it can work against you.

You know that old saying they taught us when we were kids, "Sticks and stones may break your bones, but words can never harm you." That's a nice concept, but it couldn't be further from the truth.

Perhaps words can never harm you if you're at the Spiritual level of Buddha, or any of the Great Enlightened Ones, but for us regular folk, I think it's safe to say that words can harm us very much.

All the bruises you got as a child have gone away long ago. But the humiliating, hurtful words that people said to you as a child, still ring in your ears.

Jeffrey@JeffreyGurian.com

Those are the things we never forget. Those are the things that stay with us. They are lodged deeply within our hearts, and they cause us to do things like doubt ourselves, abuse ourselves, and sometimes even hate ourselves.

I was always the smallest, thinnest, youngest looking kid in my class. Because I started school when I was only 4 1/2 years old, and then skipped the eighth grade, I looked very immature compared to most of the other kids, especially the girls. I was still only 16 when I started college.

Because some kids have no qualms about pointing out other kids' defects as they see them, I was very quickly made to feel inferior on many levels, and began creating defense mechanisms for myself at a very early age to shut out the pain.

I remember every summer for years, as a young kid, either wishing, or maybe it was even praying, that I would get to be as big as my Dad who was a six foot,

225 pound bruiser, who didn't take anything from anybody.

For some reason, I always thought it would happen over the summer, when many of my friends went away to camp, and came home many inches taller. They seemed to magically "shoot up" over the summer months. I always waited for that to happen to me.

That wasn't in the cards. Instead, I took after my mother, a small, slightly built woman. I foolishly held that against her for many years, as if she purposely had something to do with that. As if I chose my own children's genetics when they were conceived.

No child can really ever understand why he or she is different than most of the other kids. The plus side of it is that it made me determined to overcome every obstacle that presented itself to me in my life, but before I could do that, I had to endure a lot of pain.

I also lived what might best be described as a fear-based existence. As a young child, I was afraid of the dark, and often had bad dreams. In a long-standing recurrent dream, I dreamt up two horribly scary men with long fingernails, who would visit me every night, and torment me, by running their sharp fingernails over my body to see if they could wake me up. I remember their names to this very day, Buntz, and Buntze-Laben.

How strange that such a young child would make up such strange, evil-sounding foreign names. I bet someone in the world knows what they mean. I wouldn't be surprised to find out they not only had meaning, but were from a past life.

For some reason still unknown to me, I was given the courage to confront my fear. I was so uncomfortable about being afraid of the dark, that I was determined to release myself from the fear, and I made myself go in the dark alone, to show myself it was okay. I still can't believe I had the wherewithal to do that as such a young child.

The next thing I did is even more unusual to me.

Even at the tender age of about 7 years old, I was trying, and learning to control my thoughts. I also had a recurrent dream about one of my grandmothers.

I was fortunate enough to have been blessed with two loving grandmothers. One of them, my Dad's mother, who we called Nana Kitty, was the kindest, sweetest person you could ever want to meet. I began dreaming that she would take me to the basement of my building where there was a big scary boiler room, and she would leave me there.

The reality was that couldn't have been further from the truth. Adolph Hitler would have celebrated the Jewish High Holy Days, and worn a Yarmulke before that happened, but I dreamt it on a constant basis, and it deeply bothered me, and made me afraid to go to sleep.

I was determined to bring it to an end, and so one night right in the middle of my dream I confronted her and said, "You're not my grandmother. This is just a dream." Just like that. I remember it clearly to this day, and I never had the dream again.

Psychologists I have since asked about this said it was highly unusual for such a young child to be able to manifest that kind of mind control, and realize I was in a dream while I was in it. However, it was that kind of confidence in my mental powers that while helping me in one way, often worked against me in another way.

The interesting thing is that also, about the same age of 7 or 8 years old, I already knew that I could take away people's pain with my hands. It came to me intuitively, and I used to do it on myself, and on my little sister Ronnie.

I remember very clearly practicing my touch, which in retrospect is a very strange, and unusual thing for a young child to do, especially when no one else in the family guides them to do that. No one else in my family had any affinity for things like that, but I just knew it was very important for me to develop a very light touch. It helped me greatly in the many years I was a practicing dentist. In those early years, I practiced often on myself, and on my sister.

If she had a stomach ache, I did a procedure I called "Jeffrey's Famous Stomach Operation", during which I took out the "bad stuff", and replaced it with "good stuff", and she felt all better. What I didn't know until many years later was that I was doing a form of what is known as psychic surgery.

It came to me intuitively, and is one of the main reasons I believe in past lives. It must have been a holdover from something I knew before. I've been told it goes back as far as Atlantis, and when I left there, I went on to Ancient Egypt as a High Priest. You can't tell things like that to everyone, because they'll look at you funny, but I feel like I can trust you! (LOL)

What I do know is that in my earlier life, in order for me to get better, and stop stuttering, I took what must have been an inferiority complex, and turned it into a superiority complex, not to feel better than other people, but just to feel even. Just so I could show up.

I remember having feelings that no one would ever want to date me. Consequently when I got dates with girls, I was never comfortable, and never understood why they wanted to be with me. I felt that no one would ever want to marry me, that I would never have children, that I would never have a career, that patients would not want me to treat them. I had every negative thought I could have about myself.

Where did I learn that from? From my "heart wounds." From things that were "taught" to me by other people around me, by insensitive remarks from strangers, and by my own interpretation of what they said, and how I thought they viewed me.

So when I say that my life has been difficult, you must understand that that is my own personal version of things, so it may not be particularly valid, or accurate, because whose life am I comparing it to anyway?

Am I comparing it to someone eaking out a meager existence in the Amazon Rain Forest, or in some Third World country? Or am I comparing it to the imaginary life I thought I should be leading as part of my "heritage", or from the distorted media image of the perfect life we Americans believe we should be leading, as created by writers on television and in the movies.

People have probably killed themselves over the discrepancy between the life they were leading, and the life they thought they should have been leading as portrayed in the media.

The truth is that my own life is the only one I'm familiar with. So by that fact alone, my opinion tends to be skewed, just by the fact that it's my opinion. It's very subjective.

It's prejudiced by my own distorted view of things, because my view is made up of my thoughts, and my thoughts are distorted by my past experience, and how I view it.

I now know that my own view has been very flawed, which means that in terms of qualifications, I'm probably not the best person to try and evaluate my own life. That's a strange realization to make.

Contrary to my own negative beliefs, life has allowed me to experience all the things I feared I would never have. But because I was laboring under the weight of my heart wounds, I often wasn't able to truly enjoy them. My fear caused me to push them away.

If you don't love yourself, how can you possibly believe that anyone else could love you? Instead you think there's something wrong with them for loving you, and you live in fear of the day when they "come to their senses," and finally leave you.

The thought of that happening is so painful, that you push them away, creating a self-fulfilling prophecy, making the feared event happen even sooner. That way you can prove to yourself that you were right, that you are truly unlovable, . . . and here is the proof. They finally left you just as you predicted they would, when in reality you never left them any other choice, thanks to your heart wounds.

When I was in my "negative" mode, I tended to take information, and put it through this bizarre filter that I kept in my head, where it got distorted, and turned around, usually to work against me, in some negative fashion.

That's a very important observation for me to have. That I have the tendency to distort information. There was a time I didn't know that fact. The important thing is that I know it now.

It's a strange thing to realize that you're probably not the best judge of your own life.

There was a time when if you asked me the meaning of life, I would have said, "Life is a series of obstacles that you have to overcome, and in between, you just try and enjoy yourself as much as possible."

But go back for a moment to my original words. I said, "I *feel* like I've had a difficult life, and had many obstacles to overcome." That's one of my main problems right there. Confusing what I feel with what's real. Just because I feel something, doesn't necessarily make it so.

That leads me to the saying "Feelings aren't facts." I didn't always know that. I certainly didn't know that growing up. I thought if I felt it, it automatically made it true.

Furthermore, it's not so much how I feel that's the problem. It's how I *feel* about how I feel. That's the real problem.

The strange thing is that even during the times I felt as though I had a difficult life, on some level I also doubted it. On the one hand, I knew on an intellectual level that many people had lives much more difficult than mine. I had only to walk in the street for a few minutes for evidence of that. Some people are asked to endure so much more than others, and their problems are obvious to the naked eye.

Yet, my own limited perspective tells me that I've had to endure so much pain. There were times in my life that the pain felt so great, I wasn't sure I could make it, but I did, and I'm that much stronger for the experience.

As the song says, anything that doesn't kill you makes you that much stronger. Every challenge is an opportunity for your growth.

Those are very powerful thoughts, and two of the affirmations I use for re-programming the subconscious mind.

For me, thought was always the key. I thought it would lead me to freedom, and happiness. I believed that I was intelligent, and had confidence in my ability to think things through, which is basically our only reasonable approach to solving a problem in life.

The problem is that if you have any intelligence at all and have been able to achieve things in your life, you tend to believe your own thoughts.

It takes a lot of work to be able to examine your thoughts objectively and see which ones may not be valid for you.

Every time we have a decision to make, we take the facts available to us, we use our past experience as a guide, we think really hard about it, and we come up with a solution that makes sense to us. It may not make sense to anyone else, but it makes total sense to us.

If you are anything like me, generally nine times out of ten, that thinking got you into hot water. It turned out that that was my biggest downfall, . . . my thinking.

Once in awhile it worked, as when I used my thinking to figure out how to stop stuttering, but all that did was give me a false sense of power. It made me believe I could solve all my problems with my own thinking, and with the power, and determination of my own mind.

Sometimes, years later, if we're lucky, and we obtain more clarity, we wonder what we were thinking when we made those earlier decisions. But hindsight is always 20/20.

My best thinking got me into all the trouble I was ever in. I didn't know then that you can not get better with the same mind that got you sick.

I will be repeating that statement throughout the book, not because I'm running out of things to say, but because that is how we learn. We don't hear something once, and learn it. We need to hear something over and over again in order to truly learn it.

In the beginning, the first time you hear something, you learn it superficially, . . . in your head. You learn it intellectually. In order to truly learn it, it has to travel to your heart. That trip can take various amounts of time depending on whose body you're in!

In order to get better you need to have new thoughts. As I said earlier, it's kind of like re-programming your hard drive with a new database.

But in earlier days, I was a victim of my past experience, and was subjugated by my own subconscious mind. It's a very strange concept to one day realize that in trying to get better, you are actually arguing with your own mind.

I was purely a product of my thoughts. What else did I have to guide me? I couldn't use *your* thoughts. Even if I could have, I probably wouldn't have listened anyway, because again, most people don't learn from someone else's mistakes.

I was particularly stubborn in those days, and always believed that I was right. "If only everyone would just sit down, and listen to me, they'd see that I was right, and then they'd do things my way." That's how I thought. I had great confidence in my thinking. Now I know, the more I think I know, the less I truly know.

Life is always about learning. They say we are born to learn the lessons we didn't have a chance to learn, or refused to learn in a previous incarnation. I'm trying to learn as much as I can, confronting my fear and "uncomfortability" on a daily basis.

When you are on a Spiritual path, you come to realize that the more you learn, the less you know. There is always more to learn. It's a lifetime process. You never graduate. If you think you've got it, you don't.

Sometimes it scares me to think about what thoughts I am holding now as truths, that will be revealed to be false, or damaging to me at some time in the future. I need to be open to that concept, and not believe something as a truth just because it makes sense to me.

So if indeed, it turns out to be true that I have had a difficult life, I now know the purpose of it was so that I could help other people with their own problems in a more empathetic way.

I heard another great saying once which went something like, "I had a long and difficult life, fraught with terrible problems, most of which never happened!"

Experiencing my own pain and heart wounds gave me the opportunity to experience what most people come to me to be treated for, and so far, I have been given the Grace to be able to overcome every obstacle in my path.

For example, as I mentioned earlier, I stuttered very badly until my second year of college. It's a terrible affliction to be saddled with. In my Sophomore year of college, I was given the Grace to figure out how to stop stuttering, and I took the next few years to accomplish that goal. I now teach others to do the same.

Although I am not a classically trained speech therapist, many stutterers feel they would rather learn from someone who conquered the problem themselves, rather than from someone who learned how to treat it from a book. No one understands a stutterer like another stutterer. That's true empathy.

Every thought we have affects us.
—Dr. George Goodheart

(notice the name!), proved that around 1964, when he came up with the field of Applied Kinesiology, which not only proved the mind-body connection, but literally proved that the mind thinks *with* the body.

The late Dr. Candace B. Pert proved in her book "Molecules of Emotion –The Science Behind Mind-Body Medicine", with a foreword by Deepak Chopra, that every thought we have produces chemicals in our bodies. It's the science behind the power of positive thinking! She proved mind-body medicine to be true on a chemical level!

I had the distinct honor of treating this eminent scientist, and I know she wouldn't mind me divulging this. We met at a Spiritual Conference and she came to me to do my Healing work on her, and to make her an appliance to relax her jaw.

She sent me a copy of her book and autographed it to me this way:

Dear Jeff,

Your device is wonderful, but YOU are way better! I probably need another session. Maybe 8/12'ish.

Until next time,

XOOX

Candace

P.S. Enjoy the book – since all is energy, anything is possible!!!

And then she hand-drew a little heart with a face on it, with long fluttery eyelashes!

I was shocked, and saddened to learn of her passing.

Dr. John Diamond, took it one step further in the mid-to-late 70's when he developed the field of Behavioral Kinesiology, which proved beyond the shadow of a doubt, that every single thought you have either weakens you or strengthens you on an energetic level.

In my own case, I had to learn to own my sensitivity, which is a great strength that often feels like a burden. Most sensitive people go through life wishing they weren't so sensitive, instead of learning to use it as the gift it truly is.

I thought it was some terrible burden, when all I really needed to do was to learn how to embrace it, and learn how to censor my life so that I didn't allow anyone in who didn't belong there, . . . especially not someone who would abuse my sensitivity, and try and either manipulate me because of it, or somehow use it against me.

People gifted with great sensitivity and positive energy are like magnets for people who need energy. We draw them in and give to them from our hearts, because we truly want everybody around us to be happy.

Not out of meanness on their part, but many of those people we draw in, and try to "fix", are not capable of "giving back." They are perfectly capable of taking, but are completely unaware of what it means to give back. Instead they drain us of our life force, until we are suffering along with them, thinking we are just too sensitive, and weak.

I used to let everyone who showed up gain access to my life, and then tried to change myself in order to accommodate them, blaming myself constantly for being too sensitive, as if I wasn't supposed to feel the pain they inflicted upon me. I was a magnet for maniacs, and social misfits, but not any longer. In those days, I could have gone to a party for the D.A.R. (Daughters of the American Revolution), and met a woman who secretly wanted to become a stripper.

You draw into your life what you put out, and so it was important for me to come to an understanding of what, and who I had become, and the energy I was putting out to the world, in order to understand the unhealthy patterns that had developed in my life, as a result of my heart wounds, which led me to faulty thinking.

During the course of this book, I will endeavor to share with you as honestly as I can some of the most difficult times in my own life, for I have found that anytime one has the courage to share something difficult to say, or something they find personally embarrassing to share, it helps them to get better.

And I too want to continue getting better and better. I am my own project. I am my own work of art, so to speak. No one can work on me but me. No one can perfect me, and take me to higher levels of consciousness, but me. I can have guides, and teachers, but I must do the work, and I am the beneficiary of that work, as well as all those who come into contact with me.

I am on that eternal quest for knowledge and truth, that once you're on it, fills you with the hunger to learn more and more. You no longer have a choice.

For as we change, everyone else in the world is a little better off for it. The Quantum Theory Of Physics states that you can not change even one molecule in the world without changing every other molecule in the world. So as we change, we change all those around us. One by one, we can change the entire world. It's exponential.

For me, I knew I was getting better when I didn't have to tell anyone I was getting better. It was enough for me to know. Even when others told me they saw a difference in me, it didn't carry as much weight as it used to, because another important lesson for me to learn was that outside validation was not the key to Happiness. I had to learn the hard way that that never works. It's totally an inside job.

HEART WOUNDS AND
CELLULAR MEMORY

FROM TIME IMMEMORIAL, songwriters and poets have written about "broken hearts", for in reality, what are most songs about? Either finding love, or losing love. And where do we feel love? In our hearts.

Certainly not in your back, your arms, or your legs. There's no other part of the body that feels Love except for your heart. Your brain can't feel Love. It intellectualizes Love, like the great computer that it is, and tries to rationalize it, and explain what it means, in tangible terms, . . . of course to no avail, because Love is not something tangible. Love is ethereal, and conceptual.

Love is the guiding force in the Universe. It is the All Powerful, All Knowing, Omnipresent Force that rules all that we know, or ever will know. Love is G-d, and G-d is Love.

That is why we can not truly know G-d with our brains, we must know Him in our hearts. We learn things intellectually starting in our brain, but in order for us to truly "know" the information, it must make that long journey to the heart, for that is where we truly learn. That is where we internalize information.

In an earlier chapter I reminded you of that childhood saying, "Sticks and stones may break your bones, but words can never harm you."

That is probably one of the most false and damaging statements we could ever learn, or teach our children. How many of you still have that scraped knee from when you fell as a child, or that bruise on your arm where that neighborhood bully punched you? I would venture to guess no one!

But how many of you still remember the insults and humiliation we all faced growing up? How many of you remember the really mean thing that someone said to you as a child? Some of us remember that like it was yesterday.

Every single time someone lied to you, broke a promise to you, misled you, or hurt your feelings in any way, each one of those hurts, or heart wounds is still lodged inside of you, for that is the concept of Cellular Memory. We will read more about this throughout the book.

For now, suffice it to say that Cellular Memory is the concept that every single thing that has ever happened to you since you were born is still lodged somewhere inside of you, . . . deeply embedded in every cell of your body, and every fibre of your being.

It's the reason you can be walking in the street, or riding in your car listening to an oldies station, and hear a song from the past, and you'll instantly remember where you were when you first heard that song, or you'll remember the boy or girl you liked when the song first came out, even if it was 30 or 40 years ago.

It's also the reason you can experience the scent of someone's perfume, and remember instantly that your kindergarten teacher wore that fragrance. And you don't have to think about it. It happens in a millisecond. Absolutely no thought is required. It's automatic, . . . like sensory deja-vu. Only with deja-vu you wonder if it really happened before, and with Cellular Memory you know for sure that it happened before. It's particularly powerful when registering traumatic events.

One of our commonalities is that we all start out as children. Children are highly sensitive, naturally loving beings, who have not yet been taught *not* to feel their feelings. Unfortunately, they, . . . meaning "we", . . . learn the hard way.

One of the reasons that all religions in the world teach the concept of "Forgiveness", is that from the very beginnings of time, people have always done things that required "Forgiveness."

People have been insulting, hurting, and killing each other since Biblical times, and probably before. We are only human, and by that very fact, we are weak. We are plagued with natural instincts, and desires that get magnified way out of proportion, as our egos try their best to satisfy those seemingly insatiable instincts, by accumulating "More."

It doesn't matter what it is, our egos tell us we want, and "need" More. When it comes to things like money, sex, and power, it seems to be man's nature not to be satisfied. Frighteningly enough, it may also be man's nature to be violent, or greedy, or slothful, or any of the other things that came to be known as The Seven Deadly Sins, . . . Pride, Resentment, Anger, Greed, Lust, Envy, and Sloth.

So we grow up being hurt by others, and it wounds us in our hearts. We keep those wounds lodged deeply within us, and even though our minds may forget that they're there, our hearts don't forget for a second. Unfortunately, those very same wounds guide us in our everyday lives.

They guide us in every choice and decision we make, and every relationship we enter into. They make us miserable, and untrusting. They make us cynical, and fearful. They make us crazy, and they make us ill. How many of us find ourselves re-creating the same frustrating patterns in our lives, over and over again? Why do we do that?

We often have no choice. Every decision we make is based upon our thoughts. That's all we have. We examine our options, we "think it through" to the best of our abilities, and then we make a choice on how we think we should proceed.

We have no choice but to make our decision based on our past information. It's all we have to go on. It's all that's on our "hard drives." We certainly can't use someone else's mind. We're lucky if we can even know our own.

It's the very rare person that learns from someone else's experience, or mistakes. Our egos tell us that we're different. We tend to think, "It may not have worked for them, but we're different. It could certainly work for us." Even if it didn't work for thousands, or millions of other people, . . . our egos tell us that it could possibly work for us.

One of the best definitions I ever heard of the word "insanity" is, . . . doing the same thing over and over again, always expecting different results.

Marcy Calhoun, in her fabulous book, "Are You Really Too Sensitive" offers one possible reason for that, and she explains it in a very meaningful way. She uses the terms "structural" and "conceptual" to describe the two unconscious ways that ultra-sensitives, (people gifted with and in touch with their sensitivity), relate to the world outside themselves, as well as to themselves.

Structural ultra-sensitives lead their lives according to the generally accepted rules of society. They live with "structure."

They do things the "accepted" way. They also have the ability to say "Yes" and "No", and they understand the concept that the word "No" is a complete sentence.

Conceptual ultra-sensitives on the other hand, make their decisions based on the information available to them *at the moment*. Not based on what happened to them in the past, but on what's going on with them at the very moment they're faced with making the decision.

At that moment, the information available to them leads them to conclude that they can try the same thing once again, even if it didn't work a hundred times before, because all the indications are that it will work this time. Not because they are eternal optimists, but just because that's how their mind works.

If they had the capability of using their past experience as a guide, they might not have made that choice, but they don't.

As children, we all learn the saying, if at first you don't succeed try, try again. That doesn't mean try the exact same thing over and over again. It means try to reach your goal a different way. You can still have the same goal, . . . you just have to try a different route to get there.

If something didn't work ninety-nine times before, what makes you think it will work the hundredth time? I certainly hope that you don't think I'm saying not to pursue a dream, or not to keep trying to manifest something, if you think you have a good idea, or something important to bring to the world.

I'm not saying that at all. It's just that if you keep coming up against a brick wall, you have to realize that you can't necessarily go through a brick wall, you may have to find a way to go around it, and that takes thought, . . . new thought, . . . the new thought I've been talking about all throughout this book, because obviously your old information isn't working.

You can continue trying to use that old information, as long as you don't care about winding up with the exact same results, because that's what you are guaranteed to get. There are few guarantees in life, but that's one of them. You can be absolutely sure that if you do what you always did, you will get what you always got.

On the other hand, history books are filled with stories of people who never gave up. They tried and failed thousands of times, but they persevered until they finally succeeded. That's a great quality to have, especially when you're working on something creative.

You know who does that best, . . . inventors, and creative people, like writers, and artists. People who want to write books, and movies, and things like that, or people who believe they have an invention that will add something important to the world.

I think I once read that Thomas Edison tried 1,600 times before he got the lightbulb to work. He was quoted as saying, he never failed, he just found 1,600 things that didn't work. Thank G-d he never gave up, . . . or you'd be reading this book in the dark, (LOL) but that's not what I'm talking about, when I talk about the need to change your thinking.

I'm talking about the person out there, (and it could be you!), who keeps having the same bad relationship, over and over again, with a succession of different people, where the only thing that changes are their names. In that type of scenario, you must eventually realize that the only common denominator in all those situations was you.

Hard as that is to admit, the others were all different people. They all lived in different places, and probably never even met each other. There's no way they could have possibly gotten together and conspired against you to make your life miserable. They didn't need to. They had *you* on their side. You were the infiltrator in your own life. You were the undercover agent working for the enemy, that snuck behind your own lines, and sabotaged your own life.

How many of us are our own worst enemies? Raise your hands high, so I can see them. I thought so!

Some of us don't need to have any other enemies, when we know we can always count on ourselves. We seem to always be available, and we never say "no" to an opportunity to sabotage ourselves, and do something to mess up our own lives.

Sometimes it's something as simple as you only have one thing to do all day, but it's a very important thing. Maybe it's at 3 or 4 P.M. and you have all day to get ready and you still manage to show up late.

And why? Because you waited until an hour before you were due, to start getting ready because an hour sounds like a very long time, if you don't take into account that showering and dressing can easily take a half hour, and then even if your trip is only 30 minutes long, you have to expect an unexpected street closure, traffic, or any other number of things The Universe may throw at you.

Time is a difficult concept for many people. That's why certain people are always late. But when you have all day to get ready and you're still late, that to me is a good example of self-sabotage.

Why do we do that? Is it fear of success? Fear of failure? Those two things are so close, it's almost impossible to tell them apart. They're like identical twins, dressed exactly alike. They have the same symptoms, and definitely have the same results. Nothing ever works out for you the way you'd like it to.

Even the simple things that seem to work for most people don't seem to work for you.

You feel like the ultimate victim of The Universe. In actuality you're not. It just seems that way. It's because *your* will is not aligned with G-d's Will.

One of the most important Spiritual beliefs, or pieces of "new information" I use to help people (and myself), is that, "If you don't get what you want, it's not because you're being punished. It's because you're meant to have something better than that, and if you got what you thought you wanted, you wouldn't be available for the really good thing that's coming to you."

The key is to have patience, because it will not be coming on your timetable. It will be coming when it's supposed to, and not one millisecond sooner. **You can**

not micro-manipulate The Universe. It's supreme arrogance to even think you can.

Those prayers to G-d, "if You only let me get this, I'll be so good, and I'll never ask You for another thing", fall into the category of "foxhole" praying. "Please G-d, get me out of this, and I'll be good. I promise." Children do that. Adults aren't supposed to do that, . . . but what are we really, but grown up children.

The concept of the "inner child" is not just some wild, made-up concept. It's real. I don't care how old you are, inside of each of you is still that little girl or boy that needs to be held, and told that everything will be okay.

Somewhere along the process of "healing your heart, by changing your mind", you will have to find that little girl or boy, pick them up, and give them the hug they need, and may have been searching for, for a long, long time.

Sometimes it's hard to believe, but every single one of us was once a tiny, helpless little infant, who depended on other people to take care of them. The way we function as adults, and how relatively comfortable we are in the world at large, has a lot to do with how good a job those people did, and what kind of values they gave us.

If we were raised, as I was, in a "fear-based" existence, and taught not necessarily overtly, but sometimes even more damaging, covertly, and intuitively, that the world was a dangerous place, we have a lot to overcome. We grow up fearing people, and situations, and it makes our lives very difficult, because those are two things that there's no way to avoid.

"Healing Your Heart, By Changing Your Mind" is about incorporating new knowledge into your life. It's about being open to new thoughts, and detaching from knowledge you already have. That takes Willingness.

Willingness is the capacity to examine another point of view you may have previously rejected, or may never even have considered before, especially if it has worked well for many other people.

Then you have to actually be open to adding it to your way of thinking. It's an even more powerful experience if it makes you uncomfortable to even *think* about doing it.

Most people try to make their lives as comfortable as possible. There's nothing wrong with that, . . . on the surface. We all create a "box" for ourselves out of which we function. That "box" represents our boundaries of comfort, . . . our "comfort zone" so to speak. Stay within that comfort zone, we'll get along just fine, and you can be in my life, but start to get near the borders of that comfort zone, and you start to make me nervous.

Your mind says to itself, "You're gonna tell me you that you might love me? How can you possibly love me? I'm not lovable."

Because you feel that people have been telling you that, and proving that to you your entire life, and at this point, you probably believe them.

These are the kind of unhealthy thoughts, and silent conversations that run through the minds of many people, who find it hard to stay in relationships.

"So if you say you love me, there must be something terribly wrong with you. You must have nothing else going on. What's the matter with you? If you could love *me*, you must really have some very deep, serious problems."

In order to have the Willingness to try and change your mind, and use new information in your life, you must work on separating from your ego, which wants you to feel that you are so smart, that no one else can tell you anything.

It wants you to feel that you have it all figured out, and that the rest of the world is just a bunch of jerks. That's why you're so "misunderstood." "It's all *their* fault." Who are they? The entire rest of the world. Can all those people really be wrong?

Always remember, it takes nothing away from you to believe in something, especially something good, that can't possibly hurt you. Let's say for example, that you are a confirmed atheist, or agnostic, but you're depressed, and miserable, and maybe even suicidal. It happens to those people too.

If someone you trusted told you that you could have an amazingly happy life, just by believing in a loving Force of the Universe, not even to call it G-d, but just to admit that there are Forces out there beyond our comprehension, that make the sun rise, and the moon come out at night, . . . that make the seasons change, or the tides come in and out, those kind of things.

If someone could actually promise you that all your misery would fade just by allowing yourself to believe that, what would possibly keep you from trying it? Stubbornness?

What are you actually giving up to say you believe in something? How can it possibly diminish you to be open to a thought like that?

It's just a thought. Who can it hurt for you to at least be open to the possibility that it might be real? What does it take away from you? Absolutely nothing. In terms of whether there is a G-d or not, it's actually arrogant to say that you know there isn't a G-d. Who are you to claim such knowledge?

Being open to a thought that has been known to help millions of people over the years, and can not possibly harm you in any way, is a key part of getting better.

It's not like I'm asking you to believe in Forces of Evil, or Satanism, or Voodoo, or any of those things that they say will only work if you believe in them. Personally, I don't even want to know about such things. I don't want that kind of information to even enter my consciousness, because I am so aware that every thought you have has either a weakening effect, or a strengthening effect on your body.

"STAR" Therapy has the ability to help change your Cellular Memory by replacing one thought with another, and defuses the triggers. It removes the negative, and replaces it with positive.

It's an accepted physical principle that two things can not occupy the same space at the same time. It's like darkness and light. You can not have both at once. As soon as you turn on the light, the darkness disappears.

If you shine a flashlight into the darkness, you can see it even more clearly. Wherever the light shines, the darkness disappears. Not only does it disappear, but it actually becomes light, which is a great visual to use when you are treating certain illnesses with visualization.

By the same token, if your head is filled with negativity there is no room in there for positive thoughts. The negativity must be cleaned out first, and then right away, before any negativity has a chance to sneak back in, we must fill every nook and cranny with positive information, and positive thought.

THE POWER OF THOUGHT

SCIENTISTS AND DOCTORS have acknowledged this concept for years now. It's the concept behind Kinesiology, or the use of muscle testing to see how things, food, substances, and basically anything we come into contact with affects us.

Try this experiment. You'll need someone to do this with, but it's fascinating. Stand facing someone, and ask them to hold out their right arm shoulder height, palm facing towards the floor. Take your left arm, and place it on their wrist, and ask them to resist the pressure as you press their arm towards the floor. The amount of strength they exhibit is your baseline indicator against which you will compare what happens next.

Ask them to think of the happiest day of their lives. Perhaps a day when their child or grandchild was born, a day they got a large sum of money, a promotion, or the day they got married. Ask them to hold that thought in their minds. Tell them to try and picture that day as clearly as possible, and to try and recall the joy they felt. While they're doing that, try and press down on their arm. It won't budge. Firm as a rock.

Now ask them to think of the saddest day in their lives. A day of loss. A day something terrible happened. You can even ask them to think of someone they dislike, a negative event, or anything unpleasant. Let them picture the person or event as clearly as they can in their minds, and when they have that picture, press down on their wrist, and it will drop like a boulder dropped off a cliff. No strength at all.

Every thought we have affects us that way. Each thought carries with it its own vibration. Happiness is a faster vibration, and sadness is slow. It's the concept behind the power of positive thinking, and the power behind the use of Affirmations to help you literally "change your mind."

Think positively, and you will manifest positive things in your life. Think negatively, and you will feel ill and weak, and manifest negativity in your life.

It's very similar to what the Indian culture refers to as "Karma." What you put out, you draw in.

Affirmations work when they are programmed into your subconscious mind, because interestingly enough, your subconscious mind can not tell the difference between fact and fiction. It can not use deductive reasoning. It believes what you tell it. If you tell it you're a loser, and you'll never amount to anything, it has no reason to doubt you.

If you tell it you're amazing, and have unlimited potential, it also has no reason to doubt you. The importance of this concept lies in the fact that it's your subconscious mind that manifests your reality. In changing your mind, we change our subconscious. We change how we react to the triggers that surround us on a daily basis, for truly we are all always being tested.

Especially before we attain some greatness in our lives, we will inevitably be faced with some test. We will be faced with some temptation to "act out" and to engage in at least one of our character defects. Most often it is the one defect that is so powerful that if we give into it, we are likely to ruin whatever we are on the verge of achieving.

PROTECTING OUR ENERGY BY CREATING OUR OWN HAPPINESS CENTERS

BEING THAT WE can control no other environment than our own, and we're lucky if we can even do that, we must learn to do two things, . . . censor our surroundings, and change the way we think.

By "censoring our surroundings" I mean we must learn to protect ourselves and our energy, by surrounding ourselves with things, and with colors that make us feel happy, creating so-called "safe spaces" for ourselves. We must do this where we live, and where we work, and I refer to these special places as "Happiness Centers".

Each of must have our very own Happiness Center™, a place where we're surrounded by things that make us smile inside, whether it's colors we like, objects or photos we like, things from our past, novelties, or in my case besides the aforementioned items, crayons, spoons of all sizes, and balloons. (To be explained further! LOL) We also need a convenient source of quiet Healing music to be used whenever we feel the need.

Everywhere we look, we should see something positive. That extends to clothing, lighting, and on down to the very minutest details, including the pattern on your kitchen paper towels. I am currently searching for a certain pattern made by Bounty that has beautiful pastel shades, and pictures of little butterflies on them. I bought up as many as I could find. Even the paper cups I use for cold drinks, must have a happy pattern on them. No detail may be overlooked.

In my case, my entire apartment is white. White makes me happy. My carpeting is white, (Yes, I'm actually sick enough to have white carpeting in New York City .

Jeffrey@JeffreyGurian.com

That's how you know I truly believe in what I'm saying!), . . . my car is white, and even my piano is white. White is bright, and I need brightness in my life. I often believe that I'm part plant. I need that much light.

I came to the conclusion a long time ago that I have what they call SAD Syndrome, . . . Seasonal Affective Disorder. I am very sensitive to the amount of light I receive. For many years, I used to feel sad and depressed all winter because it got dark so much earlier. I say, "used to" because that doesn't happen to me anymore.

Now I honor my need for brightness and light to help me flourish, and I stay happy. I have also learned to be able to "feel the feelings" and not allow them to overwhelm me. I can have a sad day, or feel lonely, and still be okay.

Once you know these things, and understand your personal energy needs, it's important that you give them to yourself. It's part of learning to honor your sensitivity.

Until I learned to do that I was a victim of my own sensitivity. My sensitivity is so great, (I have been told by accredited psychics that I am a true empath), that it felt like a weakness instead of the great strength it truly is.

There was a time in my life that if I was with you and you were sad, I was sadder for you than you were. I over-felt my feelings. I drew in feelings like an antenna draws in radio waves.

Besides light, I also need bright, happy colors around me, which is one of the reasons I always keep brightly colored balloons all over the floor of my apartment. It's really hard to feel sad when you're surrounded by brightly colored balloons. Balloons are a sign of Happiness. You never see balloons at a funeral!

My windowsills are lined with toys. Small things I picked up in my travels. Little collections of seashells from beaches I've visited. Things that make me happy on a subliminal level. Things that make me smile inside.

Then there are my collages. I have two huge collages that I made when I was about sixteen years old. They are two of my most prized possessions. I'm amazed that I still have them. I'm amazed that I ever even *made* them, because when you're sixteen, unless you're a true artist, you're usually not home making collages.

They're framed, (thanks to an ex-girlfriend's brother), and hanging in my apartment, one in the living room, and one in the bedroom.

I remember assembling them in my best friend Jeffrey's apartment. There are many things in my life that I don't remember, but I remember very clearly the image of me being down on the floor trying to assemble all the images I cut from magazines and newspapers that I glued on these poster boards. I had them hanging in my room unframed, all throughout my teenage years.

I even "schlepped" them with me to Philadelphia where I went to Dental School, and when I got married right after Dental School, they stood in various storage spaces, until my wife and I bought a home. Then they stood in a basement storage closet getting warped for about 15 years or so, until I wound up needing my own apartment in New York City. But it wasn't until about 1990 that they were rescued, repaired, and framed to hang in my apartment. People seem to love looking at them, and they make me so happy.

They have very strong images of the 60's, and of a world that no longer exists, but also of a world that was changing rapidly in a very exciting way. On one of them, I glued a milk container, which doesn't look like any milk container we have today. I had clouds made out of cotton, some of which fell off around 1990, and many unusual comedic images of things I still use in my life today.

There's a man with a third eye, smoking a spoon. Lots of spoon images, and all the fingers, especially the thumbs, . . . are wearing hats. I can't explain my fascination with hats and spoons, and images like that, but they have stayed with me all these years, and still do today. I guess my collages prove that I've had them for most of my life.

The most amazing thing about them is an image on the one hanging in my living room. I'm sure you all remember being kids, and learning to draw a picture of a house, with a chimney, and smoke coming out of it, and trees, and grass and birds, and flowers, but what was always in the upper left hand corner??? That's right, . . . the sun. A half circle of yellow, with rays coming out of it.

On this particular collage, I used a large circle cut out of a newspaper to represent that sun. It wasn't until I mounted it in 1990, and got to see it close again that I realized that the piece of newspaper I used from the New York Times, . . . when I was sixteen years old, . . . just happened to be from the real estate section, for the block I'm living on NOW!!! How could that even happen? It shows listings for all of the East 50's and Sutton Place. How amazing is that? Twenty-five years before I moved here, I had already chosen my spot.

Even more amazing were the rents. One bedroom apartments on Sutton Place for $195.

I can only imagine what my parents must have been paying in the Bronx, if the most exclusive neighborhoods in Manhattan were only charging $195. for a one bedroom, and about $315. for two. Rent in the Bronx must have been free. I have a friend who's paying $5000. a month for a two bedroom apartment down the block from me on Sutton Place right now.

Now I'm wondering why my father didn't move us to Sutton Place in those days, or even to any place in Manhattan, when it was so reasonable. There's a thought I have to let go of. I know now, . . . and this is a very important concept to grasp, . . . that if I had changed even one thing in my life, especially where I lived growing up, I wouldn't have the life, or any of the things in my life that I treasure now.

That concept is key to be able to grasp. That's why I can never understand people who divorce, and who hate each other, . . . especially if they've had children together.

If you love your kids, always remember that they would not be those kids if not for the other person you had them with. It had to be their DNA mixed with yours that made those children. I will always be grateful to my ex-wife for the gift she gave me.

That's such an important lesson for me to learn . . . and to keep learning, and reminding myself of constantly. Every single thing in your life, . . . even the things you wish you could have changed, . . . happened exactly the way they were supposed to. I guess we were just supposed to be living in the Bronx in those days! (LOL)

Still, it never ceases to amaze me that of all the pieces of paper in the world to use to make the sun, . . . the symbol of life, . . . I chose to use one that would predict where I'd be living twenty-five years later. Obviously with what I know now, I was being guided. I take that as a very strong sign that I'm living in the right place.

All these things, and so many more which will unfold in the pages of this book, are important to making your life a happy one, making your home a true "Happiness Center ™", and creating a wonderful place for yourself to live, . . . including kind of a "daycare center for your inner child."

Along with creating our own Happiness Centers, we also need to learn to play more. As a society, we have actually forgotten how to play, and have fun. There was a time in our lives when it was natural and intuitive. Remember as a child how much fun it was when your friends would come and call for you to see if you could come out to play? Why did that ever stop? We grew up and thought we had to get serious. I truly believe that's why as a society, we're so crazy about sports.

WHY WE LOVE SPORTS

WE GET OFF on watching other people play *for* us, instead of playing ourselves. And we appreciate them so much, we pay them exorbitant salaries to do what we don't let ourselves do anymore, . . . play, and have fun.

You don't think every sports star secretly thinks it's hysterical that he gets paid millions of dollars a year to play a game that he loves? And when I use the generic "he", I'm referring to women also. Believe me, Serena Williams is laughing as loud as the men, . . . if not louder.

Not everyone can be good at sports, but there are other ways to play, just like we did when we were kids. Boys and girls alike used to color with crayons. We used to build model airplanes, until the 60's when kids realized they liked the glue more than they liked the airplanes.

We used to play ball. Rubber bouncing balls made by a company named Spalding, that we called "Spaldeen." Those little pink rubber balls that even girls had so they could play the "turning over" game. You know like "A my name is Alice, and my husband's name is Al . We come from Alabama, and we sell apples." And you'd go through the entire alphabet that way, while bouncing the ball, and crossing your leg over the ball without banging into it. If you banged into it you were "out!"

Girls jumped rope, and played games like "Pottsy". We had all kinds of street games, that I'm sure no longer exist, except maybe for stickball. What happened? We grew up and got much too serious.

Except in *my* comedy films, you never see CEO's of corporations skipping or hopping down the street. But you do see lots of them playing golf? Do you know why? Because golf is a "safe", socially acceptable game to play. It's playing . . . in a "legal" sort of way. Plus you can be competitive, and not look like "some jerk who never grew up!" They're still just playing, but they don't realize it. It's an accepted game for adults.

The problem is that somewhere along the way, also without realizing it, we lost the connection to our inner child, and we're suffering for it.

<u>FEAR</u>

MANY OF US lead what I refer to as "fear-based" existences. That means we are confronting fear on a constant basis, some of us more than others.

As very young children growing up, many of us weren't taught that the world is a safe place. Consequently, many of us wake up in the morning in fear. Almost as soon as we realize we're awake, the fear sets in. Our hearts beat fast, our stomachs start churning, and we begin waiting for the first bad thing of the day to happen.

If you haven't been given the gift of security as a young child, this is a very hard lesson to unlearn as an adult. Watching the news on television, and reading the newspapers does little to take away our fears, when almost everything you read about and see is about people killing, or maiming each other for a variety of distorted and disturbing reasons.

I grew up in a time when children were subjected to the fear of nuclear war with Russia. We had drills in school where we were told to hide under our desks, as if that would protect us during a nuclear Holocaust. The fear was all around us.

Today is little different. We're constantly being programmed to think that the world is a dangerous place, and that thought is being reinforced by so much that we see around us. You can't stand in the subway without fears of some maniac pushing you in front of a train. You can't drive on the roads without having to fear being the target of someone's "road rage". You have to be careful that your children aren't molested, even in school or at religious study.

Everywhere you look there's reason to experience fear. People are suddenly put out of work, they leave their house and have an unexpected accident, or even in the supposed safety of their own home, they can have an untoward event. Statistics say that most accidents occur in the home.

It's important to realize that every time you make either a left or right turn, your whole life is different because of it. When you leave your house, and walk either to the left or to the right, everyone in the world is in a different position depending upon which way you go. But you can't try and second-guess your every move, or dwell on things like that, or they'll drive you crazy.

The important information to keep in mind is that whichever way you choose to go is the way you were supposed to go, in order to experience whatever you were meant to experience in this life, as a learning experience. We're all here to learn lessons we haven't learned in a previous existence. When we're finished learning, we leave, and go back to wherever it is that we came from.

The experiences I mentioned above are everyday experiences, but our fears go much deeper than that. They are what we call "existential fears", having to do with our very existence. Basically no one knows why we are here, why we were born into the families we were born into, in the country we're in, with the person we're involved with, in the job or profession that we find ourselves. There are Spiritual answers to all these things, which can be comforting if you allow yourself to accept the information and keep it with you.

We supposedly choose our families before we're born in order to learn lessons we haven't finished learning in a previous life. All the frustration, and all of the obstacles that we face during the course of our lives are supposedly learning experiences, from which we become stronger, as we seek to align ourselves with G-d, and use our Faith to help us get through the difficult times.

Always remember that faith is the exact opposite of fear. Where there is faith, fear can not exist. If your faith is strong, it will keep the fear away. But sometimes, even though our faith may be strong, the fact that we're human makes us weak, and the fear creeps back in.

We must do things every day to strengthen our Faith, because we're surrounded by Fear every day. If you go to the gym once, you don't leave with the body you've always wanted. It's a process. A very gradual process.

As I tell patients I treat who stutter, or who suffer from Depression, or addiction, if you stutter, or you get high every day, you must do something to counteract it every day, not just when you feel like it.

FIGHTING THE FEAR

INSIDE EACH AND every one of us, no matter how old we may be, is a little child that still needs to be held, and needs to be told that everything is going to be all right. Many of us didn't get that as children, and so we need to learn to do that for ourselves as adults. We need to learn to visualize that little boy or girl inside of us in our mind's eye, pick them up and hold them, and tell them that everything will be just fine, and that they're safe.

Too many of us led fear-based existences, because we weren't given that security growing up. We weren't taught that the world is a safe place. I know that I certainly wasn't. I had to watch every move I made. "Watch out, don't trip, . . . look out, you'll bang your head, . . . don't run too fast, you'll fall, . . . don't walk too fast, you'll hurt yourself, . . . don't lift that, it's too heavy, . . . don't go out, it's too cold, . . . don't eat so fast, you'll get a stomach-ache, . . . don't play in the snow, you'll get sick, . . . you're not dressed warm enough, you'll catch pneumonia, . . . don't stay up too late, you'll wear yourself out, . . . don't eat that, it's not good for you, . . . don't drive too fast, you'll get killed, . . . don't do that crazy dance, you'll throw your back out, . . . don't wear your hair like that, people will think you're crazy." I could go on and on.

I wasn't allowed to cross the street by myself until way after the other kids in my neighborhood. I was kept in a crib until I was six and a half years old. I remember getting my first two-wheel bike from my grandfather, and I climbed out of my crib to see it.

Ordinarily you wouldn't remember getting out of your crib for anything, . . . you were supposed to be too young to remember, . . . but it's entirely possible if you were six and a half years old. I was told it was to save space. They needed the crib for a sibling who was yet to be born. The bottom line was I was kept in a crib much too long.

I still say my mother would dress me today if I let her. She'd put out my clothes, fix my hair, make me breakfast, and send me on my way. All out of love of course!

Fear is a killer. Over-protection can be as damaging as under-protection. We start out, as I did, by being afraid of the dark, and let it expand to being afraid of everything. It can get to the point where we're afraid to answer the phone, or open the mail.

Every time the phone rings, we expect bad news, and every piece of mail has the potential to change our lives for the worse. What a way to live.

I confront my fears on a daily basis. Fear is like a schoolyard bully. If you can gather up the courage to stand up to it, it slinks away. Fear is the opposite of Faith, and they can not co-exist, just as in the case with darkness and light. One can not exist in the presence of the other.

When you have true Faith, there is no Fear because you know in your heart that you are being guided, and protected. When I am experiencing Fear, I know that my Spiritual connection is not strong enough at that moment. I then must pray for the fear to be lifted, and must work on increasing my conscious contact with G-d through further prayer and meditation.

NEVER REGRET THE PAST
(It's Okay to Look Back,
Just Don't Stare)

I USED TO think that when you really "got it down", in other words, when you got life down to a science, and you understood what life was all about, you'd learn the knack of having everything work out perfectly. That kind of thinking is dangerous. It allows you to believe that when things go wrong, there was something you could have done differently that would have changed the outcome.

Sometimes there might have been something you could have done differently, but most of the time, it happened exactly the way it was supposed to.

The fact that we as people think that "had we only done 'such and such', we could have manipulated the situation differently, thereby causing things to work out in our favor", . . . is one of the greatest causes of stress-related illness in the world. It's also very ego-centric behavior, . . . telling ourselves that we have the power to make things go our way.

Basically, there's only two ways that things can go, . . . your way, or G-d's way. Now every once in a while, these two things may coincide, and it will seem to you like you're getting exactly what you want. It's when you try and go against G-d's Will, and try to enforce your own will that things start to get a little "hairy."

If you learn to start every day by asking to be shown what G-d's Will is for you that day, you'll start to be able to differentiate between what is your will, and what is G-d's Will for you. If G-d's Will is for you to have something other than what you have planned, you can stand on your head and do cartwheels, and absolutely nothing will work. YOU CAN NOT MICRO-MANIPULATE THE UNIVERSE. It's arrogant to think that you can.

You can go through the machinations of trying to control your life, and everything and everyone in it. It may even seem like it's almost working, because sometimes, the thing you wish to obtain may seem like it's about to happen, but then at the very last minute, it slips through your fingers, . . . like trying to climb a smooth glass wall, with nothing to grip on to, and with Vaseline on your hands.

You can not bribe G-d, or manipulate G-d into doing what you want by begging, or promising to be good, or by any other means.

G-d's Will is G-d's Will, and that's all there is to it. Every once in a while it may coincide with your will, and when that happens, you can consider yourself lucky. You'll feel like you got what you wanted.

Otherwise you must pray to be willing to accept whatever it is that's G-d's Will for you. In other words, you may as well ask for G-d's Will, because like it or not, that's what you're going to get anyway!

Even if someone you know is sick and you want to pray for them to get better. How can you assume that you know what G-d wants for that person? It's a supreme arrogance to try and tell G-d what to do. Certainly pray for that person you love to get better, but add the "tag" line, "if that is Your Will for them," or "Let it be Your Will."

You can, and certainly are supposed to take action to try and get the things you think you're supposed to have, but if you don't get them, . . . it's not because you're being punished, or that you're the Ultimate Victim of The Universe, . . . it's because G-d's Will for you is to have something else. Just accept it. You'll be much better off. You can't fight The Universe. Don't even try. Try and wear life like a loose garment!

I don't even like to use the word "try", because "try" inherently means that you are leaving yourself a way out. You are automatically opening yourself up to failure. Try not to use the word "try". See I did it again. It's such a deeply ingrained habit. Do NOT use the word "try". *Just do it!!!*

Also, learn to be kind to yourself when you make a mistake, and don't beat yourself up for it. You always did the best you could, whether you knew it or not.

OUR NEED TO PLAY

UNDERSTANDING THE NEED to play is key in changing your life, but first, . . . THE TEST!!!!!!!! (Don't be nervous, you're not being graded, . . . except by yourself!)

1. When was the last time you went into a stationery store, bought a coloring book, and a huge box of crayons, . . . and invited a friend to come over to color with you?

2. When was the last time you got ready to leave the house, and took some interesting little thing with you that would make you smile when you saw it?

Jeffrey@JeffreyGurian.com

3. When was the last time you bought some brightly colored balloons?

4. When was the last time you wandered through a toy store looking for something for yourself? Maybe something that reminded you of your childhood that would make you smile inside to own it?

5. When was the last time you bounced a ball? . . . Remember the days when you'd bounce a Spaldeen ball like I mentioned previously, or play punchball, handball, stickball, hit the penny, or even the "turning over" game I also mentioned before.

6. When was the last time you went into a stationery store, in early September to look at school supplies? I used to go in and "smell the books", especially the hard cover ones with the black and white design on the outside, to try and catch a scent that would take me back to when I was a kid.

7. And when was the last time you changed something about your own personal style, or wore something you considered so daring, that other people just had to notice you?

I could go on and on, but I think you get the point. For most of you, the answers to these, and other similar questions would be either "never", "too long ago", . . . or, "I haven't done that since I was a kid."

My own personal answers would be:

1. I carry crayons in the glove compartment of my car, as well as a game of jacks. I may not use them for years, but I love knowing that they're there. I'm sure the guys in my garage all think that I have little kids.

2. For something interesting to carry in my pocket, I often use those little tiny spoons they give you in ice cream shops to taste a new flavor. I find unusual ways to incorporate them into my activities during the day.

One thing I did as a joke was to carry a broken, or bent spoon, and told people I opened a spoon repair shop, and that I'm so busy I had to take some of my work home with me.

My coffee table at home has small interesting things on it. Among them are two "spoon plants". They're actually just flower pots with an assortment of spoons sticking out of the earth, as if they're growing. People are fascinated by them.

In general, try and say or do something you think no one on earth has ever said or done before. That has always been a goal of mine.

For instance, I ask certain visitors to my home to sign an egg. It's a good use for old eggs instead of throwing them away. I still have one from 1988.

I've had people who have signed an egg for me come up to me years later, and remind me of it. They never forgot it, because no one else had ever asked them to do something like that before. On the whole, people are not used to signing eggs. Therefore, those are the things we remember. Things we've never done before.

3. My apartment is always filled with brightly colored balloons, and I have a bag of them which I replenish regularly.

4. I walk through toy stores all the time. My apartment is filled with little "toys", and interesting items I've collected over the years.

5. I keep an old Spaldeen ball in my drawer. It's so dead, it won't even bounce, but it's a nice memory jog whenever I come across it.

6. I still smell the books in card stores, although every once in a while, I must admit, I look around first to make sure that no one's looking when I do that.

I only look around when I become self-conscious, and let my old thinking take over. When I get caught up in the concept that I'm an adult, and adults are not supposed to have fun anymore, then I let it make me feel self-conscious. It's just old time thinking and conditioning.

If I'm not careful, I can still get caught up in the fact that I'm an adult, . . . and a doctor, . . . and a daddy, . . . and that maybe people will think I shouldn't be doing these things. I do them anyway, because they make me happy, and they keep me young.

7. I look and dress in my own personal style. I've experimented with my appearance, and had fun with it. I know what it's like to have very long hair. There was a time not too long ago that I had hair like a rock star. I've worn red, or even flowered glasses like Elton John. I'm as comfortable in leather, as I am in black tie. No one could tell what I do by looking at me.

People often think I'm in the music business, and I love that because I hate stereotypes. I hate when you can look at someone and know what they do because of the way they look. It's too predictable. It's more than that, . . . it's boring. Have some fun with yourself.

THE POWER OF
CELLULAR MEMORY

A GREAT DEAL of my Healing work, including the work I do with Stutterers, has to do with Cellular Memory. The easiest way to explain Cellular Memory is to say that every single experience you've ever had since you were born, . . . and some people say even *before* you were born, . . . is encoded inside of you. It's in every cell, and in every fibre of your being.

Actors often try and tap into their cellular memory purposely, to help them with their craft. They refer to it as "sense memory", and they use that to try and help them recreate a feeling, whether it be sadness, fear, anger, or Happiness, trying to remember a time, or event in their lives when they experienced that feeling.

The difference is that true Cellular Memory doesn't require any work, or forethought. It just happens. And it seems to happen more, and more powerfully when revisiting a trauma.

If you have experienced either a physical or emotional trauma, and even years later find yourself in similar circumstances, either physically or emotionally, your body and mind will respond the way they did during the original event.

For example, people who have survived a violent attack, may experience feelings of fear and anxiety even by walking near an area that reminds them of the area where the attack occurred. It's a very common occurrence in Post-Traumatic Stress Disorder.

Or if your significant other broke your heart, and moved to 23rd Street, every time you are near 23rd Street, or even hear the words "23rd Street", you may experience a feeling of overwhelming sadness, or even some kind of physical reaction.

You can even feel it if you travel past a restaurant where you used to go together, or if you even hear just the beginning of a song you shared. Each one of those things acts as a "trigger."

The interesting thing is that at some point from doing the kind of work I'm describing, you can still experience the trigger, but it does NOT have to elicit the same response.

I have not stuttered in many years, but I have been in situations where I felt like I could, if I let myself. If I am in a room filled with people at a meeting, and someone suggests that we go around the room quickly to introduce ourselves, that is the worst situation for a stutterer.

Not only the fact of having to say our name to strangers but to do it "quickly", makes it even more intense. So I experience the trigger, but then I look at each and every person in the room and I ask myself who am I going to give my power away to? Who am I going to let make me feel so "less than" that I feel the need to stutter FOR them.

Then I get angry, . . . not at myself or at the other people in the room, . . . I get angry at whatever it is in my mind that would let me slip back into something so terrible, and I REFUSE to stutter. When it comes my turn, I speak loudly and confidently, and most important, . . . fluently. Without stuttering, because I no longer have any need to stutter.

As a young teenager, I was forever turning off the radio as soon as I heard the song, "Bobby's Girl", because I lost my first serious girlfriend in high school to a guy named Bobby. Years later, I heard they actually got married. At least that made me feel better, . . . but it took many years for that to happen.

I must have been 14 or 15 years old at the time. Her name was Celia. She was voted the prettiest girl in her class, because we did things like that in those days. She went away to camp the summer we were dating, and I was supposed to go and visit her. My Dad tried to drive me up there to visit her on our way to the mountains on vacation, but he got lost on the way, and we never got there. I always blamed him for that.

In the interim she met this guy named Bobby and that was it. I always felt that if I had made it there that day, things might have been different.

I have the feeling that that experience started me on the path of always feeling that just before I got somewhere that I really wanted to be, or accomplished something really important, that something unexpected would happen to stop me from either getting there or stop me from achieving my goal.

You see, when we left our house that day to make the trip, there was no discussion of the possibility of not getting there. We were committed to getting there. So maybe it was the fact that my Dad just gave up, and didn't keep trying to find it that bothered me the most. He was the kind of guy that hated asking anyone for directions. And of course there was no GPS in those days. If you couldn't find it on your own, you couldn't find it!

But the point is it happened all those years ago and I can still feel the disappointment of not getting there that day. A few weeks later, I got the letter from her that changed my life, and taught me that I had the tendency to be obsessive in my thinking. She had met someone new, and felt the need to write and tell me that she didn't feel the same about me anymore. I can still feel the sinking feeling of sadness I felt that day, all those years ago.

I couldn't stop thinking about her, and how it could have been different, for a very long time afterwards. I tortured myself by walking past places that reminded me of her. I couldn't think of anything else but trying to get her back. It never happened. I was devastated.

I always wondered how it would have turned out if we had actually gotten to her camp, and I had had a chance to see her again. I carried that pain for many years, and the truth be told, if I try really hard, I can think of it now, and remember sitting in the back of my Dad's car, when he told me we had to stop looking for her camp, and I can still feel a tiny twinge of sadness. That's how powerful cellular memory is.

USING "VERBALIZATION" TO CHANGE CELLULAR MEMORY

WHEN TREATING PEOPLE for either chronic depression, or chronic pain, it's important to realize that they usually live in a world of negativity. They interpret everything that happens to them in a negative way. They take information, and run it through this filter that exists in their minds. It distorts the information, and usually turns it against themselves. They never experience feelings they interpret as "good" or "pleasurable." They don't allow it, and very often they don't even feel they deserve it.

They block themselves from experiencing pleasure.

A great part of my Healing work is done with touch. Touch is the most powerful of all the five senses as far as I am concerned, and as a society in general, it's the one we feel least comfortable with. Touch is very misunderstood, and often abused, which is why it's misunderstood. Touch is very intimate, and often carries a sexual connotation, which also makes us nervous.

One of the problems is that as a society we're obsessed with sex, and we hate ourselves for it. It's a simple fact, and I'll go into it in more detail later. Suffice it to say that as a society, we can't emphasize sexuality in advertising and entertainment, the way we do, and then make people feel guilty for thinking about it.

But for now, let's talk about touch. Touch can be pleasurable, and that's okay. Pleasure is not a dirty word. Some of my Healing work feels like massage. I explain to patients that at certain points during the process I may ask them if something I'm doing feels good to them, and if it does, it's not enough to just shake your head "yes", or say "Uh-huh", registering an affirmative answer.

Such a short, non-committal answer can be overlooked by the person who said it. You can actually ignore your own statement.

I need them to say, "Yes, that feels good to me", because when they hear themselves say those words, it registers in their subconscious, and also in their consciousness, that they have experienced something pleasurable.

It's an entire sentence. They can't miss that they said it. They have "allowed" themselves to experience something they felt was pleasurable, and they have acknowledged it.

Most chronic pain sufferers never allow themselves to experience anything pleasurable, and certainly don't interpret it that way even if they do. They say things like, "Yeh, it's okay." "That's not bad". I want them to be able to say, "That feels really good", or even "that feels amazing," because I teach them that there are no limits as to how good they can feel. The only limits are the ones they create for themselves.

What happens is very similar to the concept of physically writing down your goals. People say that there's power in the physical act of writing, as opposed to just thinking about, or mentally formulating your goals.

Writing them down, imprints them into your subconscious mind, and it's your subconscious mind that creates your reality. Your subconscious mind can not tell the difference between fact and fiction which is why Affirmations can be so powerful, and are a big part of my approach to re-programming your mind, and your whole way of thinking.

It's the basis behind the concept of Positive Thinking. Why are our thoughts so powerful? Because your subconscious mind believes you. If you think you're nothing, you will be nothing. If you truly believe you're great, you can be great.

MAKING YOURSELF "THE PROJECT"

ONE OF THE things I treat is stuttering. As I mentioned in the introduction to this book, I was a very severe stutterer until my second year of college, when I made the conscious decision that I was going to do whatever I had to do to stop stuttering, because I absolutely refused to go through my entire life with that burden.

I realized that I had the power to do that, because I realized that when I was alone I could speak perfectly. I only stuttered when YOU were there.

That told me that there was really nothing wrong with me, because a true disability is not affected by your location or who you are with. A man with a limp, limps in every room of his house. He can't go into a room by himself and stop limping. It's a true disability. My stuttering was not.

It just made sense to me that if I could speak perfectly when I was alone in a room, . . . which most stutterers can do, . . . but I stuttered when *you* were there, then it had to have something to do with how I felt about myself in front of you. It had to be coming from my mind, as opposed to being a physical problem. I was determined to change that.

It took me about two or three years, as I recall, to work through my own technique, and make a major difference in my speech. Basically I took an inferiority complex, and turned it into a superiority complex, not to feel better than other people, but just to feel equal.

It was a form of auto-hypnosis, or auto-suggestion, but I wound up basically brainwashing myself into understanding, and believing that I no longer _needed_ to stutter.

Changing something so dramatic takes commitment, and lots, and lots of work. I was literally obsessed with stopping stuttering.

But making yourself a project, and making a dramatic change in yourself in some way, should be an exciting thing to do, because you are the direct beneficiary of the results, and the outcome brings you to a higher level of consciousness, and understanding.

I have come to look at stuttering as a very deeply engrained habit, triggered by Cellular Memory as it pertains to trauma or the re-experiencing of an uncomfortable event. The similarity of how this event makes you feel, to how you felt as a child in similar circumstances, is the trigger that brings about the stuttering response.

Most stutterers started stuttering as young child-ren, . . . but well after they began to speak, and probably as a sub-conscious reaction to what was going on in their lives at the time.

I believe it is a subconscious "decision" that your mind makes in response to certain events that are occurring in your life at the time you began to stutter. No one ever says to themselves, "I think I'll start stuttering now."

However, there are only a finite number of habits that people engage in as a response to stress, and if you try and list them, you'll be able to think of a few, but the list is far from endless. You have:

- Nail Biting

- Eye Twitch

- Fidgeting

- Hair Twisting

- Picking at your skin

- Tapping your foot

- Smoking

- Drinking alcohol and taking drugs (I understand these as addictions, and as a disease, but some people might place them in the category of stress-related habits)

- Cutting yourself

- Clenching and grinding your teeth

Add any more that you can think of. The point is that it is not an unending list. No one has their very own personal habit that no one else has. No one jumps up into the air and spins around like a top, in response to stress. There are only so many things that a human being can do. I believe that stuttering is one of those choices.

I also believe it's not important to try and determine exactly what caused your stuttering. That could take many years, and you're not guaranteed to ever really come to any definitive conclusion about it. However it's VERY important to examine the possibilities, and see which ones may pertain to you.

It may have been a cry for attention, or a way of rebelling against perfectionism, or it could be many other things, but the important thing to know is that it is not a physical defect. There is nothing physically wrong with your speech mechanism, and you don't have to continue stuttering forever.

You'll stop when your mind is ready to let you stop, and not one second before. The concept here again that it's important to grasp, is that you are literally arguing with your own mind. Your subconscious mind truly believes that you need to stutter.

It not only wants you to stutter, it *demands* that you stutter to appease it. When it realizes that you want to stop, it gets nervous, and tells you things like you're wasting your time, you're wasting your money, you have better things to do, stuttering isn't so bad, . . . all the "bull" you need to hear to keep you stuttering.

When the day comes that you are finally ready to stop stuttering, you can bet that you will be scared, because as much as you hate it, it's been a part of your identity for so long, that it will make you nervous to give it up, . . . because who will you be if you don't stutter?

Where Cellular Memory comes in is that when you are in a "traumatic" situation, or any stressful situation which makes you feel the way you did as that young child, who "needed" to stutter, your Cellular Memory kicks in, the same as it does when you hear that old song, or experience the scent of that perfume, and it triggers that subconscious choice you made all those years ago to stutter as a response to what is happening. Again, no thought is involved. It's immediate, and automatic.

The important point to realize though is that, . . . it's no longer a valid response! What scared you as a child, should no longer have the same effect on you. It may have been a valid choice at the time, but not any longer.

Just as you would not be attracted as an adult to the same person you may have had a crush on as a twelve year old, you should not let a feeling you had then affect you now the same way either.

This type of thinking has helped me to make sense out of my own life. I always wondered why my life had to be so difficult. I've gone through many painful, trying situations, with so many obstacles for me to face, and I now know that it was so that I could take my wide range of experiences, and heart wounds, and use that to help others.

That is truly what life is meant to be about. Gratitude, and service. Being grateful for what we have been given, and doing service to others to "give back", what we have been given so freely. At this point in my life, it makes perfect sense to me.

CHANGING YOUR PERCEPTION
OF THE EVENTS THAT
OCCUR IN YOUR LIFE

I'VE TITLED THE following story "The Ultimate Victim of The Universe". When you read it, you'll see exactly why!

"THE ULTIMATE VICTIM OF THE UNIVERSE"

It was Monday morning, May 31, 1994, my first day back at work after having been away for more than a week. The reason I remember the day exactly, is because

I wrote it down so I could never forget the lesson I was about to learn.

I had been looking forward to coming back to work for many reasons, mostly because I enjoyed my work, but also because I was looking forward to seeing my newly reupholstered office furniture, which was sent out the day I left, supposedly reupholstered while I had been away, and replaced in it's original position about a day or two before I came back.

I awakened with a start, and glanced over at my alarm clock, which I kept near enough to me to be able to hit the snooze button comfortably, without having to stretch too far.

For the first moment, I just thought my eyesight was blurry because I could have sworn it said 8:57 A.M. I knew that couldn't be right, because I set the clock myself the night before for 7:15 A.M.

And even though I always keep that clock ten to fifteen minutes fast, for a person like myself who needs a good hour or so to get ready in the morning, I knew intuitively that ten, or fifteen minutes was certainly not going to be enough time to get up, shower, get dressed, eat something, and drive a half an hour to my office in The Bronx, where I had a 9:00 patient scheduled.

So I blinked my eyes a few times, fully expecting the clock to go back to the correct time it was set for, 7:15 A.M., knowing in the recesses of my mind, where I keep the keys to my comfort zone, that it was really about 7 A.M., as I said, because I always kept that clock set fast.

Imagine my horror when I saw that the clock had changed, but not in the way I expected. It was now 8:58 A.M., and I had in fact a minute less than I had before. I jumped up with a start, thinking the first thing I should do when this is all over is to sue the clock company for making defective clocks that allow people to oversleep, because they don't go off when they're supposed to.

That was before I realized that I had indeed set it for 7:15, but I set it for 7:15 P.M., not A.M., and so I really had no grounds for my earth-shattering lawsuit.

I immediately called my office ready to explain to my nurse why I would be detained. I was sitting in traffic on the highway, and couldn't budge. The only problem was that no one answered my office phone. That couldn't possibly be. I redialed once again, only to get my own voice on my answering machine asking me to leave a message for me. It was now about five after nine. I ran inside and tried to think. In a panic, at about 9:10 by this time, I called my nurse's home, and to my increasing horror, she answered the phone. This was getting worse by the second. Even faster than that.

I blurted out inelegantly, "What are you doing home?", and she explained to me that she was sick. This after just being out for more than a week on vacation while I was away. Rather than having my office ready for me for my return, sorting my mail, and being there to help me through the first day back, which is always the roughest day when you've been away, she decided to stay home, without even calling me. I fought to stay calm and contain myself.

At that moment, my call waiting goes off, and I excuse myself for a minute, mostly to try and gather my thoughts. On the other line is my other nurse, who I was praying would have opened the office when the two of us weren't there on time, but she had forgotten her keys and was locked out in the street with the 9:00 patient.

She said to me, "What are you doing home?" I couldn't even begin to tell her, because I couldn't really grasp the significance of what was going on. All I felt was pure, unadulterated panic setting in.

I told her to buy the patient some coffee, and I'd reimburse her, not waiting long enough for her to tell me she had probably forgotten her wallet as well. I told her I'd be there as soon as I could. I went back to call waiting, and told the first nurse what happened with the second nurse, and she didn't even sound that upset, which made me even more upset.

I washed, dressed, and ran out of the house like a maniac, grabbing my new little puppy, which I had been hoping to train to stay with me at the office all day, kind of like a companion. He was too little to leave at home alone all day, as he needed to be walked, and still wasn't really housebroken, and when you're foolish enough to have white carpeting, you really can't be too careful.

I get to the garage, and there's a crush of people waiting for their cars. I slip the guy a few bucks, and tell him I'm in a big hurry, if he wouldn't mind getting me my car asap. He brings the car around. I throw my things inside, and put the little pup, . . . a yellow Lab, . . . in the back seat. Before I even had a chance to go around to the front to get in, this little pup Max, lets go with a combination of inappropriate bodily fluids, and relieves himself all over my beautiful leather upholstery.

At this point, I'm losing my mind. Absolutely losing my mind, and I'm holding up traffic, because they brought my car around in front of other people, and now I'm not pulling out, and other people need to leave and go to their own destinations.

I know I can't drive this way with the dog sliding in and out of his own mess. I was so distraught, I wanted to either throw out the dog, or throw out the car, but the last thing I wanted to do was to start cleaning out this mess at what was now 9:27 in the morning.

Luckily, they had some paper towels in the garage. While holding Max back with one hand, I started trying to clean up this incredible, disgusting mess, while at the same time, trying to discourage him from the idea that this was part of a game. I think he thought that every time I leaned in with a paper towel, I wanted to start playing with him, cause he kept jumping up to grab the paper.

By this time, he had the mess all over his paws, so he was putting it back as fast as I was cleaning it up. I took him out and put him in the garage office for a minute, so I could clean without being attacked.

I got to my office about 10:00 A.M., grabbed my briefcase in one arm, the dog in the other, and ran to my door, only to find that my nine o'clock patient had left, and my nurse was still locked out in the street with a new emergency patient who needed immediate care.

I opened the office, and immediately knew something was strange. It looked empty. It wasn't supposed to be empty. It was supposed to be filled with my newly upholstered office furniture, ready to accommodate the rear ends of all the wonderful patients who were waiting to come in and see me.

Then I thought, "I know, maybe they piled the furniture in another room." I ran in there, . . . no furniture. No furniture anywhere. It was SRO, standing room only, and not because I wanted it that way. Plus, the office was boiling hot because it had been closed up for the last ten days or so.

I brought the emergency patient a folding chair I found in the back, to sit on, and ran over to turn on my water cooled air conditioner, which suddenly made a strange choking noise, and then began shooting streams of water out of a pipe that I guess needed to burst, at that exact moment, shooting streams of water all over my beautiful new carpeting.

This couldn't even be happening. I've seen stuff like this happen in movies, but not in anyone's life. What sort of Karmic debt was I paying off to endure this type of punishment? I knew I must have done something really horrible in a past life to have a morning like this, but it wasn't even over yet, because as I frantically searched for the valve to turn off the water that was quickly ruining my new carpeting, and that the dog was playing in, again thinking that this was a game, I found two dead mice in my reception area that must have come out of the walls, and died from the heat, right where everyone could see them.

To tell you the honest truth, at that point, I felt like lying down right next to them, and joining them. What stopped me was that I heard the buzzer go off, meaning that my nurse had seated the ten o'clock patient that was waiting to see me, besides the emergency patient that was waiting for me on the folding chair.

As I entered the room where the patient was seated, this lovely middle-aged woman looked over at me and sweetly said, "Good morning doctor, and how was your vacation?", and all I could say was "Great, Mrs. Barron, just great!"

What I learned from that day was many things. First of all, I made it through. In retrospect, I'm glad I didn't kill myself, because I've had many wonderful times since then that I never would have had if I had killed myself.

Secondly, none of those things was that important. As incredibly stressful as that day was, I wouldn't even remember it now if I hadn't written it down right then, and the only reason I did that was because I knew I'd need it some day to help other people by using it as an example of a day when everything went wrong.

Once again, the point is that in the scheme of things, it really didn't matter. What matters is if you have your health, and you and those you care about are okay. All those other things seem important at the time, but really aren't, in the big picture.

REPROGRAMMING YOUR
MIND THROUGH THE
USE OF AFFIRMATIONS

THE "A" IN "STAR" Therapy™ stands for "Affirmative." Affirmations are brief positive statements, meant to be repeated over and over again, to help you "change your mind", and create a new way of thinking.

My apartment is filled with positive affirmations that I create for myself. They contain messages and information that I need to incorporate into my life. I write them, and then have them printed in the colors of the Chakras.

They say things like, "No Obstacle Can Stand In My Way", "Fight The Fear", "Every Challenge Is An Opportunity For My Growth", "I Can Accomplish Anything I Put My Mind To", "Where There Is Faith, There Is No Room For Fear", and "There are No Limits But The Ones You Create For Yourself" . . . all highly positive messages. I put them all over. Everywhere my eyes can wander. Every single place I can possibly direct my gaze during the course of my day.

As I pass by them throughout the day, I read them without knowing that I'm doing so. Your mind absorbs the messages they carry on a subconscious, or subliminal level without you having to do anything special, or specifically stop and read them.

It's important to repeat the affirmation at least 15 to 20 times in a row, to help imprint the message into your consciousness. You cannot overdo it. It's kind of like brainwashing yourself, so the more you can repeat them during the course of the day, the better.

First you imprint the information into your subconscious mind, which interestingly enough, automatically accepts the affirmative message as a truth, since as I've mentioned several times already, your subconscious mind can not tell the difference between truth and fiction.

Eventually the affirmative message works its way into your conscious mind. But it's important to know that your subconscious mind creates your reality. It creates the world that you're living in, and *that* is the mind that needs to be changed with the help of the "new information" found in this book.

I also use affirmations in my cure for stuttering to help re-program the way you think. Stutterers must be willing to re-program the way they think, in order to combat the fears that keep them from being fluent, and that stop them from raising their self esteem, and owning their personal power.

They must be taught new concepts, . . . that the control of stuttering lies within them, and that they're actually fighting with their own mind when they decide to stop stuttering, because it's their mind that made the choice to do it in the first place.

Most if not all stutterers know that when they go into a room by themselves, they can speak with absolute fluency. They can say every single sound that they have trouble with when they're speaking in front of other people, and they can speak with absolute confidence.

The frustration of knowing that, is one of the most helpful things in helping them to stop stuttering, because it should prove to them that there is absolutely nothing wrong with their throat, their vocal chords, or anything else about their speech mechanism. The problem is in their mind. There's no other part of your body that makes decisions, . . . not your back, your neck, or your leg. It all comes from your mind.

That's why in order to get better, you almost have to detach from your mind. In this case, your mind is your enemy. In order to get better, you have to <u>fool your own mind</u>. You have to prove to your mind that you no longer need to stutter, no matter how hard it tries to insist that you do.

I realize that to the uninitiated, these may sound like strange concepts, . . . and they should, because that's what makes it new information. If you already knew it, it wouldn't be considered a new way to think.

It's critically important that the person who stutters realizes that they have a choice, and that they'll be perfectly okay, even if they decide to stop stuttering. That will all be explained later on, in its own chapter.

Suffice it to say that when I was working on my own cure, I was obsessed with stopping stuttering. I created affirmations, and said them to myself literally hundreds, and hundreds of times a day, in order to deeply engrain them into my subconscious mind. Just like engraving the grooves into a record, . . . if anyone out there actually still remembers what a vinyl record looked like!

GOING TO ANOTHER LEVEL

WHAT DOES THAT EVEN MEAN?

(INCLUDING THE SALVADOR DALI STORY)

VERY OFTEN, I'LL use the term "going to another level" to explain what you need to do in your mind, in order to allow you to do something you would ordinarily find it difficult to do, whether it's trying out for an acting part, making a speech to a large group of people, wearing an outfit you consider kind of

Jeffrey@JeffreyGurian.com

daring, or having the courage to initiate contact with a person you find interesting.

It's almost like leaving your body, and becoming someone else for a few minutes, . . . preferably someone who's not nervous to do the thing you fear doing.

I have personally used that technique in the past to be able to do things like stop stuttering, or show up at certain appearances that would have made me nervous had I not gone to another level, or even to meet certain celebrities, who were difficult to meet, but who I felt the need to exchange energy with on a one-to-one basis.

In my early life, there were only a few people I ever really wanted to meet, and using the technique of going to another level, and detaching from my self-consciousness, I was able to manifest a meeting with each of them.

This eclectic mix of people included Woody Allen, Salvador Dali, The Beach Boys, and Deepak Chopra, an unusual mix if they were all to be in the same room together!

I have always felt that I could arrange to meet anyone I set out to meet, by "owning" certain principles, and by allowing myself to go to another level. For the purposes of brevity, I'll include only one story now.

THE SALVADOR DALI STORY

I was married and living in Scarsdale at the time, when I decided it was time to meet Salvador Dali. His work was just so amazing to me, especially "Melting Watches", and I felt that he would definitely "get" what I was about, and we'd become good friends. Another delusion of mine.

I had been reading the New York Post since I was a kid, when I used to dream about being in Earl Wilson's column, a goal I actually achieved on more than one occasion. (I'm sure I'm dating myself with that reference.) He was the precursor to Cindy Adams.

Anyway, I read in the Post that Salvador Dali would be staying at the St. Regis Hotel, on East 55th Street in

Manhattan. I wasn't aware until that point in time that the St. Regis was a regular haunt for him when he was in town. I had never planned to meet him before.

At that time, I had bought my first car, . . . a brand new 1975 Mandarin Orange Eldorado that supposedly had been made for one of the Isley Brothers, who, as the story was told to me by the dealer, had changed his mind after he ordered it. The car was as big as a boat. I had customized it to look like the cars the pimps drove in those days in New York.

It was a regular "Pimp-mobile", with a Rolls Royce grille, huge white wall tires, a white Cabriolet roof, those ornamental straps on the side that usually only hearses have, and a CB radio that was made to look like a telephone. Cell phones had not been invented yet!

At that point in my life, I wanted to be SuperFly. I used to play that tape non-stop when I was driving. Of course it was an 8 track in those days. I would cruise around Manhattan, and when I would drive on the West Side of town, the hookers would all check out my car, as would the pimps, the drug dealers, and the cops. The kicker was, I had D.D.S. plates on the car.

The worst thing about my orange Eldorado was that my poor wife had to drive that car around Scarsdale. She often said to me,

"Why do we have to have an orange Cadillac? The other women in the neighborhood make fun of me." She didn't get it.

The car made a statement. Not a statement I'd particularly like to make today, but back then that's where I was at. I used that car to make things happen. I used that car to help me have fun, meet interesting people, and to get a lot of things, . . . even to get up to Saturday Night Live, . . . but that'll be a story for my next book!

So, it was mid-afternoon that I pulled up in front of the St. Regis hotel. It must have been a Wednesday, because that was always my day off, and I always spent that day in the city. So I pull up in front of the hotel in this shiny orange Cadillac Eldorado, I throw the doorman a few bucks, and casually say, "Please watch my car for me. I'll be back soon, Salvador Dali's expecting me." He says, "you're in luck, he just walked in."

I went into the lobby assuming that all I had to do was ask the desk for Salvador Dali's room number, but it doesn't work that way. They weren't giving out any information on Mr. Dali, and I realized I had been very naive, to think I could just walk in and see him.

I went back out to my car, saw the same doorman, and in a moment of inspiration blurted out, "Are you sure you saw him go in, 'cause I just called his room, and they said he's not there." To which the doorman replied, "Are you sure you dialed the right room . . . room 1023?" And now I had the room number! Amazing!

So I went back in and called, expecting to have to go through at least ten people before I reached him, but lo and behold, he answered the phone himself. After recovering my composure on realizing I was actually speaking to him, I told him that we had met before, that

I was a surrealistic dentist whose specialty was putting the back teeth in the front and the front teeth in the back, which made for a highly unusual smile, and that he had told me to call him when I was in New York again, knowing that he probably meets so many people, he'd never remember if this was true or not.

He cut me off by saying, "Sunday night at 7 P.M.", and with that he hung up.

I was kind of confused by the abruptness of the conversation on his end, but I took that to mean that he wanted me to come down to the hotel that Sunday at 7 P.M. Either that or it meant to get out of town by Sunday at 7P.M., but I chose to believe he had invited me down.

That Sunday night about 5:30, my wife sees me getting dressed to go out, and asks me where I'm going. I casually say, "I'm going to meet Salvador Dali."

I basically tell her the story, and she in all of her wisdom, . . . and in her case I really mean it, . . . she says, "What are you going to tell him if he asks you why you're there?" I assured her that that would never happen, but just in case, I took two red plastic spoons with me, and my "thumb-hats", which I'll explain to you next.

When I was about 16 years old, around the time I was making my "famous" collages, one of my first girlfriends, a girl named Danni, did me the honor of making me tiny hats for my thumbs, by cutting up her mother's artificial fruit. By seeing my collages, I can tell I was already into the concept of "thumbhats". I'm not really sure why, . . . it just appealed to me.

One thumb got a tiny bowler, by cutting an artificial grape in half. For the other thumb, she actually crocheted a lovely pink hat with a tiny flower. I still have both of them to this very day. They're in the box with the spider that looks like W.C. Fields, (my favorite comedy star of all time!) that she also made for me.

She was so into my humor. I wish I knew where she was. She would be absolutely shocked to know that I still had these things today. They're one of my most cherished, and treasured possessions. I had always hoped to run into her again someday, but as yet I haven't. I hope she's well. (Since this was written it has come to my attention through an amazing synchronicity on Facebook of all places, that dear Danni has left this plane and made her transition way too young. R.I.P. Danni!)

Anyway, I grabbed the spoons and the thumbhats, and left my poor, confused wife to go and meet Salvador Dali. I got there early, and parked close by the hotel. After having told one of the doormen that I was there to meet Dali, but didn't know where to go, I was informed that whenever Dali was in town, it was kind of a ritual that he would hold court in the King Cole Lounge of the St. Regis, . . . and that he usually makes a late entrance.

I found out that there was only one elevator bank that came down from his room, so I parked myself in a comfortable chair across from the elevators, figuring I would wait there until he came down, and I'd meet him right away. I remember hoping that I would recognize him. I needn't have worried.

As I sat there, I began noticing a very strange assortment of people starting to show up, and filing into the King Cole Lounge. The two that stick out most in my mind were a girl with basketball weights tied around her arms and legs, and a French dwarf, who must have been an artist, and who showed up carrying a huge black, leather portfolio filled with his work.

When Dali finally stepped out of the elevator, there was no chance that it could have been anyone else in the world. Nobody ever looked like that before or since. He was carrying a jeweled walking stick, and wearing a full-length mink coat in August, and his moustache went all the way up in the air on the ends. He was amazing.

I immediately walked over and introduced myself, and for some unknown reason I spoke to him in Spanish. It was at that point that the most amazing thing happened. He acknowledged me, and then totally disacknowledged me if there is such a thing, and he walked down the corridor towards the King Cole Lounge without so much as even a glance towards me, or seemingly knowing I was even still there.

I remember feeling embarrassed, as I ran beside him, feeling sort of like a little, yapping puppy, trying its best to get its master's attention. He didn't answer one word I said to him. He totally ignored me. I remember wondering whether I should just leave, but I didn't.

I followed him all the way into the King Cole Lounge, and all the way to the back of the room, to this really long table, at which he stopped, and suddenly, from this place of totally ignoring me, he began introducing me to everyone who was there as if I had been his son. He put his arm on my shoulder, and started telling everyone about me. It was the weirdest thing, because up until that point, I had been thinking that I should either just kill myself, or leave.

We went to sit down, and he ushered me into a seat just two seats away from him. He sat at the head of this huge table, with one person next to him on his right, as

I remember. On his left was one other person, and then me, and across from me was Geraldo Rivera, who was still pretty new in those days, but was already popular. I remember wanting to know him also, but we didn't really get a chance to connect that night.

There was only one other "known" person there, a blonde socialite whose name I can't remember. It was a very long table of people, all of whom had some reason to be there. We ordered tea or coffee, and as I recall they served desserts.

Suddenly to my horror, Dali announced that one by one we would go around the table and tell everyone else why we were there. My wife was such a witch! (In a good way! LOL) She knew everything. The only thing I recall about the rest of the group, was some people opening up a line of surrealistic clothing that they wanted to show him. When it got to me, I definitely had to go to another level in order to say what I was about to say.

I told the group in a very serious way that I used to be a surrealistic dentist, and told them about the back teeth in the front thing, but that I had changed careers and now I manufactured "eye-spoons", which most people found very relaxing to use. As I said that, I inserted one of the small red spoons into my eye like a monocle, and began speaking about the depth of relaxation one could achieve with such a method.

I had created the "eyespoon" thing in Philadelphia, while I was in dental school, around 1970, during a visit from my old pal Tommy R. who came down from the Bronx, via Morocco.

Tommy wore red swimmers' goggles most of the time in those days, and for some reason I realized that I had the ability to hold a plastic spoon in my eye, for long periods of time, while having conversations with people, and acting as if I didn't even know it was there. It was a wild week-end, to say the least. That was the week-end that "Spoon-eye" was born.

Many years later, Conan O'Brien tried to claim it as his own, but with the help of T.V. commentator/columnist Cindy Adams, I set him straight on that point. She actually wrote about it in her well-read column in the NY Post.

As a quick aside, I remember walking through Central Park by the fountain where everyone hung out in the early 70's. Every Sunday afternoon, people would show up looking as wild as possible, basically just trying to "freak each other out!"

I was walking casually with a spoon in my eye, as I passed one of Andy Warhol's legends, . . . it could have been Ultra Violet, who had covered herself in Vaseline, and as she passed by she looked over at me and I heard her say to her companion, "Holy S*@%, that guy's got a f*&#-ing spoon in his eye." Even SHE freaked out over Spoon-Eye!

Anyway, I knew in my heart that there was nothing I could possibly say that would ever freak out Salvador Dali, and I was right. As I had the one spoon in my eye, he took the other spoon from me, and tried to stick it into his ear. I told him it was only for the eyes. He asked me to put the other one in also, and I told him if I did that, I wouldn't be able to see anything, and he said that was alright, . . . he just wanted to see me with both of them in.

I did this for him, and the entire table of "eccentrics" and "unusual people" were laughing at me. They're laughing at me because they think *I'm* strange. Talk about having to go to another level. By the time I took out the thumb hats, and told him that I also manufacture these, I think he was ready to go on to the next person.

One of the things I remember most about that magical evening was how Dali controlled who sat near him. At one point, a beautiful girl came in with her boyfriend, and he had someone else move so the girl could sit next to him, while he put the boyfriend at the other end of the table. He kept me right where I was, . . . right near him.

When the evening ended, he summoned a waiter who brought him his full-length fur coat, and he chose two people to come with him somewhere else. One of them was Geraldo, and the other was the woman I can't remember. I want to say it was either Cornelia Guest, or Candy Bergen, but I'm not sure why.

I left, and got into my mandarin orange Eldorado, and almost intuitively, found them walking in the street. I pulled up next to them, and offered them a ride, but they said they wanted to walk and enjoy the evening. They probably just didn't want to be seen in a customized mandarin orange Eldorado. Anyway, that was how going to another level gave me my magical evening with Salvador Dali.

As an upshot to this story, fairly recently I was at a social event where people were taking pictures of me, and a well-dressed Black man in his 50's approached me and asked me who I was. I believe he was carrying a walking stick of some kind.

I told him I'd tell him who I was if he told me who HE was and he introduced himself as one of the Isley Brothers, to which I blurted out, "I had your car!", and told him the story.

Without a moment's hesitation, he said, "That was my uncle Marvin's car. I remember the car exactly." And then I told him where I had bought it in The Bronx, at which point he hugged me and said, "Now I know you're on the level because no White man ever bought a car there!" And we both had a good laugh!

It took over 35 years to get verification of that story, but it just proves that The Universe will eventually answer every question you ask of it!

THE QUEST FOR
KNOWLEDGE AND TRUTH

B UT THE CONCEPT of going to other "levels" also applies to how you lead your life. One of my own personal goals has always been to try and lead my life on many levels, and to try and raise my level of consciousness to the highest level imaginable. Now some of you will understand this statement immediately, and others will say, "What the heck is he talking about?"

I'll assume that if you're reading this book in the first place, you will intuitively have some knowledge of what I'm talking about. Unfortunately, and I don't mean this in a judgmental way, . . . just as a fact, . . . most of the world leads their lives on a very superficial level.

They live within the first three Chakras, representing things like money, sex, and power, never looking for more insight into life, than those basic things to sustain them. And there's nothing wrong with any of those things, as long as we take them to higher levels. At least to the level of the Heart Chakra.

But then there are those of us who want to know more. Not even by choice, . . . we simply *need* to know more. It's beyond our control.

Some of us realize we were just born to that path. We have been given an insatiable craving for knowledge and truth that comes from deep within us. A craving that just will not let us rest until we not only acknowledge its existence, but also honor it, by trying to absorb as much esoteric wisdom as possible.

That craving, which started in me as a very young child, is another one of the things that convinces me of past lives. Not having parents who had any interest in

Healing, or esoteric wisdom at all, it always strikes me as odd that as a young child of only 7 or 8 years old, I was already practicing my touch.

Even at that young age, it was important to me to develop as light a touch as possible. That is a highly unusual thing for such a young child to do, unless it's a carry-over from a previous existence.

That type of beginning made it easier for me to seek out a life lived, and experienced through my Heart Chakra. As you try and raise your level of experience and live your life at the level of the fourth Chakra, . . . the heart, . . . you begin to *feel* more, which is probably the thing that scares most people. You begin to get in touch with the sensitivity that we were all given, but block ourselves from embracing.

So often sensitivity is mistaken for a weakness, instead of the strength that it really is. Hopefully I have covered that subject in my discussions on Sensitivity, but suffice it to say that allowing yourself to experience the beauty of your sensitivity, by living through your heart, is a goal of anyone who wishes to live their life on a higher level.

THE IMPORTANCE OF OWNING YOUR SENSITIVITY, AND DETACHING FROM SELF-CONSCIOUSNESS

ANOTHER WAY OF going to a higher level is to detach from self-consciousness. People who feel the touch of my hands invariably tell me how warm they feel. They've been described to me as feeling like heating pads. Even in the winter.

The reason for that is that I am a tactile person. I relate to the world through touch. For so many years, I've been so used to touching people physically, both as a dentist and in my personal life, that I am totally un-selfconscious when it comes to touch.

This allows me to stay in touch with my heart, and to transfer the warmth from my heart into my hands. When people experience that warmth, they should be able to intuitively tell that I honestly care about their well-being.

Owning my sensitivity and my power, allows me to do that without feeling threatened by them knowing that. So when I run into you in the street, and give you what I think is a big, warm hug, I'm hoping you can tell that I'm genuinely happy to see you.

All too often, we're afraid to let people know that we care. Many of us didn't get that growing up, so to get it from an acquaintance, or from their doctor can be an overwhelming, and unsettling experience for them. It's the reason that many patients are moved to tears during a Healing session, . . . especially if they've been able to energetically release past abuse from their hearts.

People can also tell whether you're being sincere, or being phony when you interact with them like that. They can tell by using their intuition. Through my work, I've learned to have the courage to speak, and act through my heart, . . . and it does take courage, . . . and when you do that honestly, people can tell. We all have the power to distinguish between people being real, and people being "phony". Sometimes, they don't mean to be "phony", . . . it's just that that's all they know.

Living through your heart is not always easy. As a matter of fact, I wondered for a long time why I was so sensitive to so many things, and why I felt things so deeply, when the same circumstances didn't seem to bother others at all.

There was a time in my life that if I was with you and you were sad, I was sadder for you than you were, which made it very uncomfortable for me to exist.

I was like an antenna for other people's feelings. It didn't allow me to be of service. I had to back away because it was too uncomfortable. It may have made it look like I didn't care, when the truth was I cared too much.

I thought I wanted to change that, until I learned that I was an empath, and that Sensitivity was one of my gifts.

I also had to learn that you can not change your basic nature. I felt like I wanted to change because it made me feel weak. The truth was I was allowing people into my life who didn't *honor* my sensitivity, and were manipulating me because of it.

I doubted myself, because I wasn't honoring the depth of my sensitivity. I was handling my sensitivity as a weakness, instead of looking at it as the great strength that it is.

People seeking enlightenment have to work very hard to increase, and to own their sensitivity, because only in doing so, can we even approach the concept of empathy, . . . trying to understand how someone else feels. If we could truly do that, the world would be a much kinder place.

As human beings, one of our great weaknesses is not being able to feel another person's pain. We can't even remember our own pain, and maybe that's a gift as well. I remember once, I dislocated my shoulder. I clearly remember thinking it was the worst pain I had ever had. The scariest part was wondering how bad it could actually get.

Would I eventually pass out from the intensity of it, or would I be able to take it? Those were the questions running through my mind, and as I had had no previous experience with pain this severe, I had nothing to base my experience on. It was all new information to me, so I had no idea what was going to happen, and that's what made it so scary.

Now intellectually, I know it was the worst pain I ever had, but I do not have the ability to recall the intensity of the experience on a physical level. We don't have that capability as people. I guess in a way, we were spared that, but I firmly believe that if we as people, had the ability to feel another person's feelings, or physical pain, we would be much kinder to each other as a species. If we could feel how it feels when we hurt, or humiliate someone else, I'm sure we would do it less often.

These days with the current focus on "bullying", and the attempt to expose how rampant it is on many levels throughout our society, this is particularly pertinent.

ACHIEVING HAPPINESS THROUGH A SPIRITUAL APPROACH TO LIFE

AS WE MOVE further into the Millennium, the world-wide spiritual movement grows stronger day by day. People are searching for answers to age-old questions. Why are we here, . . . what's life all about, . . . is there any rhyme or reason to the Universe, . . . is there a G-d? All these existential questions. And the one concept that's most important to grasp is that, if there is a G-d, and I truly believe there is, . . . it's important to know it isn't you!

You are not the one who makes the sun rise every morning, and makes the moon come out every night. You are not the one who rules the tides, or creates storms, or droughts, or avalanches. And you are not the one who has the final say on what happens in your life.

It's the belief that there exists a power greater than yourself, that controls the events of our lives, that is the basis for Spirituality. Whether you refer to that Power as G-d, or Nature, or the Universe, it's all the same thing. I, personally, feel more comfortable calling that power G-d.

Not the "old man", punishing "sky-G-d" that I learned about in my youth, but an all-knowing, loving presence, who often does things that we can't possibly comprehend, mostly because we're only human, and can't understand G-d's plan for us.

All we have to know is that after we take whatever actions we think we should take in our lives, we should sit back, and leave the results up to G-d.

Spirituality is very different from religion, as I explained in Chapter 3, "The Difference Between Spirituality and Religion." Religion is great, and I respect everyone's religion, but religion tends to divide people, by putting you in a category. It puts you in a certain group, and by definition other people not of your religion, are outside of your group. It can be seen as "exclusive."

What Spirituality does is bring people together, on the basis that we're all here together under the guidance of forces beyond our comprehension. It's "inclusive."

Next time you're walking in the street, look at the faces of the people coming towards you. Notice how few of them look like they're happy, or even have a pleasant expression on their face, or even show a tiny hint of having a willingness to smile.

Most people look like they once smiled many years ago, then thought better of the idea, and swore never to do that again. They project total negativity. Look at your *own* face in a mirror, and see what you project. Are YOU one of those people?

I look at people's faces all the time. As an inveterate people watcher, sometimes I can't believe how many people have to pass by in the street, before I see someone that looks really happy, . . . that just gives off that positive glow.

Some people's faces are actually locked into a permanent grimace, as if they were still experiencing some trauma from their past. Their faces are contorted, frozen in fear or despair, or however they reacted to that traumatic event.

I see them coming towards me, and I can't believe it. It looks like a scene from Michael Jackson's video "Thriller." I know for sure that they didn't always look like that.

It's obvious that they've taken a particularly hard knock in life, and never let go of it. They kept it with them as a reminder, so that just in case, one day, they should almost forget how miserable life is, all they have to do is look in the mirror to be reminded.

We've all heard the saying, "You can either look at the glass as being half empty, or half full." Looking at the glass as being half full leads us to our next topic, . . . Gratitude.

GRATITUDE

GRATITUDE IN LIFE is key. It's one of the hardest things to learn, because it seems to be human nature to take things for granted. It wasn't until I had severe back pain for four months, and learned to get used to walking with a limp, that I learned a lot about gratitude.

I had always known the concept, but it was really brought home to me, when I finally got rid of the pain and the limp after four months of working with a chiropractor and then a Healer.

Jeffrey@JeffreyGurian.com

After the pain was gone, I thought of how many years previously I had had no back pain, no sciatic pain, and didn't have to walk with a limp, and never, . . . not once, did I ever wake up expressing gratitude for my legs, and a painfree back. Never did I stop and think how lucky I was to be living a pain-free existence. But when I had that pain, I longed for the past when I had been pain-free.

Some people have no legs. They've lost their legs, and what they wouldn't give to walk with a limp. I had a limp, and I knew I couldn't dare to feel sorry for myself, because with G-d's Grace, my limp just might go away, . . . which it did, but not before I learned that great lesson.

Now every single day, when I awaken and express my morning prayer of gratitude, I always include the sentence, ". . . and thank you G-d for another day without pain." I'll never again take it for granted that I am supposed to have a life free of pain. That circumstance can change at any given moment.

I experienced it again recently after undergoing the pain of passing a kidney stone, which the textbooks say is the worst pain you can have, comparable to childbirth.

At least with childbirth you get a baby out of it. All I got was a heart-shaped stone. (True fact!)

The moment it passed after six hours straight of intense pain, which felt like my insides were being squeezed with a wrench, I immediately went to a state of Gratitude, which I actually recall each day. I never want to forget how lucky I am to have a day without pain, when that can change in a moment's notice.

And as soon as the pain was gone, I tried injecting some humor into the situation. I happened to have had an umbrella with me, and always carry a small camera, and just before they released me, but while I still had the I.V. in my arm, I opened my umbrella, and asked the patient in the bed next to me to take a photo of me in my hospital bed holding the open umbrella. It's a very funny photo and drew quite a bit of attention from the staff!

The fact that I have all my senses, and they work, . . . the fact that I have a nice place to live, a family that loves me, two beautiful children, a mind that always gives me inspiration, a few good friends, and enough money to pay my bills, is so, so much more than most people in the world have, that I must be grateful for those things every day.

Mostly because there are no guarantees that came with my life saying that those things are either my birthright, or my inalienable right. Those things are in my life as a result of the Grace of my Higher Power, who again, I feel comfortable calling G-d.

I've learned that when I don't get what I want, or I lose something, or someone dear to me, that for whatever reason, that's what G-d's Will is for me. Obviously it's not *my* will, or I would never have let it happen. So who else's will could it be?

If we don't come to the conclusion that it's the will of a Higher Power, . . . a force beyond our comprehension, . . . the thought that we are actually in control can literally drive us crazy. Because then we wonder why things don't work out better, or work out just the way we want them to, even when we try and micro-manage our lives?

Our mental health depends on us being able to grasp the concept that our lives are under the control of a Higher Power. We must also grasp the concept that you never lose <u>anything</u> you're supposed to have, and that if you don't get what you want, it's not because you're being punished, or are "The Ultimate Victim of The Universe", and that nothing ever works out for you!

It's because you're supposed to have something *better* than that, and if you got the thing you wanted, you wouldn't be available for the really good thing that's coming to you.

The problem is that means we have to have "patience" and human beings are not good at having patience. From the time we're little we cry when we don't get something we want. We cry and scream until our parents give us what we want. And we want it immediately. Not later! We want it now!

If we're not careful, we grow up to be adults that respond the same way, kicking and screaming our way though life every time something doesn't go the way we want it to go.

So when you can truly take the above-mentioned concepts into your life, and not only intellectualize them, but actually internalize them into your heart, you will take all the stress out of your life.

You'll understand that you should definitely take the action of trying to achieve every single thing you want in your life, but if you don't get it, just know that something better is in store for you. The key once again is to have patience.

Patience is necessary because you have no idea when that "good thing" is going to happen, and that's where the faith comes in. The concept here is "Don't Stop Before the Miracle Happens".

When you know in your heart, . . . not 100 percent, but 1 _million_ percent . . . that wonderful things will eventually happen, . . . that amazing things are in store for you when you really have that faith, . . . then you can afford to wait, and be available, so that not only are you able to recognize the opportunity when it comes, but you're also able to take advantage of it.

SERVICE

THERE'S A WONDERFUL concept that says, "You can't keep it unless you give it away." The "it" in that sentence can either be Peace, Serenity, Happiness, a feeling of Centeredness, or a "One-ness" with The Universe. The important thing to know is that by sharing it with others, you make it stronger in yourself.

One of the ways of experiencing this in your own life is by doing service to humanity expecting nothing back for yourself. It's the principle of doing three unselfish acts of kindness every day for people you don't know. I was going to use the term "perfect strangers", but you'd never be able to find any, . . . because nobody's perfect!!! (LOL)

It could be something as simple as helping one of those foreign delivery guys on a bike, pick up a food delivery he dropped all over the street, . . . or holding the elevator door for someone rushing to make it, instead of making believe we don't see them, . . . or just having a smile for someone who didn't expect it, and may not get one from anyone else that day, . . . or simply acting polite to all people who cross our paths during the course of the day.

You'd be amazed at the difference this makes in your life, and the lives of others, because of the number of people who actually do cross our paths each day. And it's exponential in the fact that everyone that we touch in some way touches someone else, so everything you do eventually affects everything, and everyone else in the universe.

It's like the quantum theory of physics, in which every electron has a cause and effect on every other electron in the universe. It's basically too vast a concept for us to grasp, . . . unless you're Stephen Hawking, . . . and even Stephen Hawking isn't Stephen Hawking, if you know what I mean!

It's like trying to understand the concept of infinity. Try and picture this. As many millions of miles as we could go out into space, . . . to the very tip of your imagination, . . . just as you reach that farthest away point that you can possibly conceive of, . . . you're actually just starting. It's mind-boggling. So it's at that point where we just have to have faith, and accept something on that basis. It's just too much for us to grasp.

Service to humanity takes us out of ourselves, and helps us to detach from our self-seeking motives. Try it the next time you're feeling down, and hopeless. Try getting out of it by getting involved in service, and in helping someone else get through the trials and tribulations of _their_ day, and watch how fast you forget about your own troubles.

WHY BAD THINGS
HAPPEN TO GOOD PEOPLE

THIS IS A question that has plagued man since time immemorial. Especially now, post September 11th, 2001, a day that has changed the world forever as we knew it, it's a question on the minds of millions.

How could there be a G-d who allows thousands of ordinary, regular, people, . . . not soldiers, . . . but run-of-the-mill people, to just go to work one day, and never come home again?

How could there be a G-d who allows things like the Holocaust, where six million people perished because of their faith? Faith is not a tangible thing. It's not like they died for doing something wrong, or for committing some crime. Their crime was just for being who they were.

They died for something they believed in. They died for basically a thought. Not for anything they did, but for a thought.

Life is all so synchronicitous, yet all so planned. I could just as easily have been born in Europe during the 1930's as to have been born in the United States when I was. Hence the phrase, "there but for the grace of G-d go I." It could always have been me.

The person born with terrible deformities, or the person I just saw in a wheelchair, could just as easily have been me.

Whenever I'm feeling particularly sorry for myself about any certain situation in my life, G-d reminds me of how grateful I should be by putting someone in front of me in a much more unfortunate situation.

Who knows why some people have to live with such burdens. The most comforting thought to me about why that is, is that they are reliving some lesson they did not get a chance to learn in a previous existence. If you were a very rich, but mean and miserly man in a former existence, you may be returned to this life as a humble beggar.

G-d doesn't punish people, as much as it might seem to the people enduring these hardships that he does.

Sometimes, life just makes no sense. That's where Faith comes in to play.

The only reason I am Jeffrey Gurian is because my parents told me I was. They gave me that name, and so that's who I became. I could just have easily been born in any other country, with any other name, because I am really just an accumulation of trillions of cells, . . . a mass of protoplasm, filled with tubes, and fluid, and bits of matter here and there formed into organ systems, that function miraculously to keep me alive.

But when I stop being alive, what then? This mass of protoplasm stops moving. The fluid stops flowing through the myriad of tubes, and I just lie there very still, but what of my spirit? My spirit is of energy. You can not kill or destroy energy.

As a person of Jewish heritage, born here after World War II, and growing up in New York City, I remember feeling tremendous fear as a child, as I'd hear adults whispering about what happened to the Jewish people in Europe.

I remember having tremendous fear over the idea alone that just because of something about you that you couldn't even see, that people would want to kill you. That is not a concept that a child can even attempt to grasp, which is why it's even more disturbing when we see video footage of young children in certain countries being taught to hate, and fire guns, in the name of their "god."

Any god that would encourage children to hate can not be the G-d we are talking about.

Children are not born with hatred. They are born pure, and with all the knowledge in the world. I truly believe that infants come from such a perfect place, that they are born knowing all the secrets of the Universe, but by the time they learn how to speak, they forget.

Infants from every country that has ever been at war with each other would grow up to be best friends if they grew up together, because all people are inherently the same.

It's the reason you can adopt a child from another country, and bring him up as your own, and the only way you might be able to tell is from physical characteristics if the child is of another race.

My sister adopted a beautiful little baby boy from Vietnam, who was just Bar Mitzvah'ed, and spoke Hebrew as good as anyone else in the Temple.

When G-d takes people we love too soon, and it always feels like it's too soon, it's because G-d is more concerned with your Spirit than He is with your body.

That one concept has done more to comfort me than almost anything else I've learned in my journey.

It helped make sense of something that always bothered me and others who I've heard ask, "If there is a G-d, then why does he allow such terrible things to happen?"

We were given Free Will, the opportunity to do what we want. Men often use their Free Will to accomplish evil deeds, and hurt and maim the bodies of other human beings. The thought that G-d is not concerned with our bodies, (which are only transient vessels), but with our Spirit, is the reason he lets certain good people leave the Earth before their time.

He needs their Spirit for another purpose. Perhaps that is why HE does not intervene at the last second to save the righteous, and the good people from devastating harm. He's there to nurture, and take care of your spirit, once it's free of the confines of your physical body.

It's the only reason to explain why good men are allowed to die in crimes, accidents, war, and illness, and of course when I say "men" I'm referring to women as well. It's too awkward to keep writing men/women, so just keep in mind that the "men" I am referring to is "mankind", not in the usual gender specificity.

THE POWER OF SMILING

A SMILE AFFECTS your whole body from the skin right down to the skeleton, including all the blood vessels, nerves, and muscles. It affects the functioning of every organ. It influences every gland. Even one smile often relaxes a number of muscles, and when smiling becomes a habit you can easily see how the effect will mount up. Last year's smiles are paying you dividends today.

The effect of a smile on other people is no less remarkable. It disarms suspicion, melts away fear and anger, and brings forth the best in the other person—

Jeffrey@JeffreyGurian.com

which "best" he immediately proceeds to give back to you.

I just returned from shopping in a super market where I was about to ask an unfriendly looking clerk for help in finding something.

I found that I judged him incorrectly because despite my concern I asked him anyway, and he greeted me with a big smile that transformed his entire demeanor, and then he went to find out the answer to my question.

A smile is to personal contacts
what oil is to machinery,
and no intelligent engineer
ever neglects lubrication.
Rejoice evermore (1 Thessalonians 5:16).

This is a direct quote from Emmet Fox's book, Around The Year With Emmet Fox.

SPIRITUAL WISDOM
TO USE EVERY DAY

SAYINGS AND APHORISMS TO GET
YOU THROUGH ANYTHING IN LIFE

Don't dwell in the past. It's okay to look back, . . . just don't stare.

Yesterday is history, tomorrow's a mystery, today is the gift, . . . that's why they call it the present.

Don't fight the universe. Why are you holding onto rhinestones when G-d is trying to give you diamonds?

All you need to know about a Higher Power is that you're not it.

The job of G-d is taken, so don't bother applying.

If you have a problem, and you can't solve the problem, chances are you _are_ the problem.

Guilt is paying interest on a debt you don't owe.

The more you say, the less people remember.

You can't get better with the same mind that got you sick!

Don't give up before the miracle happens.

Don't mistake self-loathing for humility.

If you think you can change your life alone, you're not in for a spiritual awakening, you're in for a rude awakening.

Your head is like a bad neighborhood. Don't go in there alone.

If you're having a conversation and you're alone, chances are it's not a good conversation.

The program of learning to lead a spiritual life, is a simple program for complicated people.

Alcoholism, and drug addiction are more often than not, a low level search for G-d.

Alcohol and drugs give you wings, but they take away the sky.

FEAR = False Evidence Appearing Real

Fear is the opposite of Faith. When your Faith is strong, there is no room for Fear. Fear and Faith can not co-exist.

The more dependent we become on a Higher Power, the more independent we become in our own lives.

Before speaking "honestly", take a moment and ask yourself—does this really need to be said, does it need to be said *now*, and does it need to be said by me?

Pain in life is inevitable, suffering is optional.

Expectation is the precursor for resentment.

Resentment is like *you taking* poison, expecting the other person to die.

The suggestions made in this book are free. The only ones you pay for are the ones you don't take.

If after reading this book, you try these principles in your life, and you're still not happy, we'll gladly refund your misery.

EPILOGUE

I'VE HEARD IT said that there's nothing new in the world. That it's all been said. That is in alignment with the statement I made early in the book that the Spiritual concept is that we're all born with all the knowledge we need inside of us, but we're not in touch with it.

We're certainly not using it, and really not even aware of it, until someone crosses our path who says or does something that puts us in touch with that knowledge, and then it's like an "Aha reaction." The information resonates with us and feels comfortable, because we realize that we already knew it all along.

So it's not so much what we learn by reading books such as this one, it's what it re-affirms to you. Sensitive people need to be re-affirmed because we tend to doubt ourselves, and the more sensitive and creative we are, the more we tend to doubt ourselves.

We also tend to feel alone and not part of, and by "we" I'm referring to anyone who would be reading a book of this sort.

We tend to see and experience the world in a different way than most people do, and so we tend not to fall into a category, which can make other people around us uncomfortable. For some reason people like to put other people in a category.

Unfortunately most people in the world are not actively working on themselves in any kind of Spiritual program, and not to be judgmental, but they tend to lead their lives on a somewhat superficial level.

Being re-affirmed by like-minded individuals is often what saves us. It allows us to feel "a part of." As if we do belong to a group of some sort. It nurtures and strengthens us, like giving water to a plant.

We also don't learn anything by hearing it once. Some of the themes in this book have been repeated in different ways, because we only learn through repetition.

As you incorporate the principles in this book into your life you will raise your level of consciousness.

As you raise your level of consciousness, keep this saying in mind. It's one of the most important sayings I ever heard, and I wish I could remember where I heard it:

"The higher up the mountain you go, the lonelier it gets, . . . but the view is magnificent!"

The higher you go, the less and less people there are on that level to share it with, but the ones that you meet will be that much more special!

And if you are mindful, you will "recognize" each other. So stay aware, open your hearts to the ones that you meet, allow yourself to release your heart wounds, and please enjoy the journey to Happiness!

ACKNOWLEDGMENTS

THIS IS A very special and meaningful book for me, and one I've wanted to write for a very long time. Maybe 15 years. Before my Dad left us back in 2001, I had been told I had a book deal on an earlier version of this book, and I was so glad I got to tell him that. Unfortunately it never came to be. But as I explain in this book, everything happens exactly when it's supposed to, and not a minute sooner.

Very recently I had the good fortune to meet an extremely talented medium who connected very strongly with my Dad, and told me some really wonderful things from "the other side." He also said he saw a book that would be very important to me and to others. It would be particularly special if this was it.

So I want to start out by acknowledging my parents, Marge and Ray Gurian for their unwavering support in everything I ever did, (and I feel that they still support me), and I want to thank my Dad in particular for giving me my sense of humor.

A big thanks to my sister Ronnie for putting up with me as we were growing up, thanks to Jane for "the girls", and to childhood friends like Jeffrey Asseo, Kenny Engelbourg, David Grossman, Danni Cruz, Steve Schwab, Nathan Oventhal, Neil Cohen, Richie Veloso, Celia Nass, Leslie Koffler, Steve Grodsky, Andy Kaufman, and close friends from later years like Todd Miller, without whose technical and computer skills I would not have been able to write.

Big thanks to people like Richie Tienken, Debbie Kessler, Ron Bennington, Gail Bennington, Chris Stanley, Chris Mazzilli, Steve Mazzilli, Emilio Savone,

Gina Savage, J.R. Ravitz, Tom-E, Jeannie Tienken, Frank Chindamo, Cris and Paul Italia, Noam Dworman, Estee Adoram, Paul Ronca, and the whole JFL crew, the people at The Stand, New York Comedy Club, Broadway Comedy Club, Gotham Comedy Club, Stand-Up New York, The Comedy Cellar, and all the people in the comedy world that make me feel at home when I'm there.

Special thanks to leaders in consciousness like Deepak Chopra, Wayne Dyer and Marianne Williamson for inspiring me, and all of whom I've had the good fortune to meet, and thanks to the Board of The Association for Spirituality and Psychotherapy, plus founding members Ken Porter, Sam Menahem, and Henry Grayson, including the late Daniel Miller, for all of their support.

And if you're reading this book at all, it's totally thanks to Jen Henderson of Wild Words Formatting for her expertise and to my dear friend uber-author Otakara Klettke for all of her help in guiding me through the maze of self-publishing.

And a very special thank you to my graphic artist and friend Ace Salisbury for his talent and devotion in designing the covers to this book.

And finally to my children, my two amazing daughters Elizabeth and Kathryn, the lights of my life. I would be nowhere without you and your beautiful families, including Dero, Nicky, Lilly, Danny, Brookie, Adri, and little tiny Tyler!

BIBLIOGRAPHY

THE INFORMATION IN this book is a compilation of all I have read, experienced, and internalized over the years, and some of the information is intuitive.

I intend to list all the books and references I can think of that have influenced me, in no particular order. Publishers are included wherever possible.

Are You Really Too Sensitive, by Marcy Calhoun, Blue Dolphin Press

You Can Heal Your Life, by Louise Hay, Hay House

Spiritual Healing, by Dr. Stuart Grayson

Anatomy of the Spirit, by Carolyn Myss, Sounds True Publishing

Ageless Body Timeless Mind by Dr. Deepak Chopra, Harmony Books

Spiritual Solutions – Answers to Life's Greatest Challenges; by Dr. Deepak Chopra

How to Know G-d – The Soul's Journey Into the Mystery of Mysteries, by Dr. Deepak Chopra, Harmony Books

The Book of Secrets by Dr. Deepak Chopra, Harmony Books

The Power of Intention – by Dr. Wayne Dyer; Hay House

Manifest Your Destiny – The Nine Spiritual Principles for Getting Everything You Want, by Dr. Wayne Dyer; Harper Collins

Power vs. Force by Dr. David R. Hawkins; Hay House

A Return to Love by Marianne Williamson; Hay House

A Year of Miracles – Daily Devotions and Reflections by Marianne Williamson; Hay House

Daily Grace by Marianne Williamson; Hay House

Really anything ever written by Dr. Deepak Chopra, Dr. Wayne Dyer and Marianne Williamson!

"The New Physics of Love" and "Your Power to Heal", by Dr. Henry Grayson, Ph.D

Made in the USA
Las Vegas, NV
24 August 2021

28841994R00136